I0019347

Personal Robots

1980-2014

(c) 2014

Patrick H. Stakem

PRRB Publishing

1st edition, 2nd in Series, Robots

Table of Contents

Introduction

This book is about the Personal Robots from the 1980's that inspired hopes for the future. This was triggered, in part, by the robots of the Star War series. R2D2 was based on the three service droids of the early Science Fiction movie, *Silent Running*. They were named Huey, Louie, and Dewey. At the same time, personal computers were emerging as affordable and easier to use. The excitement and the technology reached a tipping point. Before this time, robotics mainly meant large hydraulic units that manufactured cars. Now it came to mean personal companions. The expectations were limitless. We will present the evolutionary path from those early products and efforts, to the projects of today.

The word robot is from the Czech *robota*, which means servant or laborer. It was coined by novelist Karel Capek in a 1917 short story. His 1920's play R.U.R, Rossum's Universal Robots, brought the term to the public eye. "Robot" was first applied to describe manipulator systems for manufacturing and the science fiction creations.

Well before that, hacker extraordinaire Leonardo da Vinci animated a suit of armor with mechanical mechanisms, drawings of which exist.

A large number of hobby-class robots appeared in the 1980s - chief among them the HERO series from Heath. In the 1980's, the International Personal Robotics Conferences provided a forum for hobbyists to get together and compare notes. Personal robots emerged as distinct from industrial (blue-collar) robots.

Nolan Bushnell, of Atari fame, described these early efforts as PC's on a p.c. - personal computers on a push cart. The advent of personal computers, first the Apple, then the IBM pc, enabled personal or hobby robotics, by providing the computation platform. The next challenge was mobility, sensors, software, and mechanisms.

The Personal Robot Industry changed focus in several directions. As it became clear that an affordable general purpose robot was both too complex technically and too expensive, the efforts of the industry and subculture were focused in other directions - service robots, with a well-defined role, and battlebots - a popular entertainment sport. Smaller robot construction kits from companies such as Lego emerged. Toys such as radio controlled cars, boats, and airplanes provided mobility platforms.

Helicopters are hard to fly, but small computers and microelectronic gyros allowed for a stable rotary wing platform at low cost. Deployed GPS technology allowed position and destination determination. Not only was the technology becoming available, but it was becoming cheaper.

In the area of software, control algorithms could be implemented in c, but Seymor Papert, at MIT, developed an object oriented language, Logo, specifically to teach programming to young children. They could control a "turtle" on the screen, or an actual plastic "turtle" crawling around on the floor, but tethered with a cable.

As Personal Robots are maturing, and the applications become more feasible as the basis technology becomes cheap and available, it is an exciting time.

Author

Mr. Stakem has degrees in Electrical Engineering from Carnegie Mellon University, and Physics, and Computer Science from the Johns Hopkins University.

He teaches and the Johns Hopkins University, Whiting School of Engineering. He has worked with numerous NASA Centers and space missions since 1971. He participated for two years with NASA's Summer Robotics Engineering Boot Camp, which resulted in a compact car-sized autonomous Rover deployed in Greenland, measuring the thickness of the ice sheet.

He participated in the personal computer revolution, building his first unit in 1975. In 1982, he built his first personal robot.

Dedication

To the community of experimenters who are working with robotic systems, just because it is fun.

This books talks about robots we own personally. It attempts to identify the sources of the advent of personal robots, and what were the technological drivers. Robots, both as servants and as unusual artifacts, have caught the imagination of people since at least Greek times. Now, th technology has gotten us to the point where we can buy or build robot units. These are not just toys, but machines we can program and operate to do work for us. It is getting easier and less expensive to participate. I always believed, compute projects are interesting, but when your project gets up off the workbench and walks off, you've achieved something interesting. Let's take a look at a recent timeline in robotics.

Time Line

Some significant dates in personal robotics.

1939 – World's Fair. Westinghouse introduces Electro, a humanoid robot.

1942 – Asimov's 3 Laws of Robotics published.

1972 - Huey, Dewey, and Louie, Service Droids, appear in the movie *Silent Running.*

1975 – IBM PC announced

1977 - R2D2 and C-3PO appear in the Movie *Star Wars Episode IV: A New Hope.*

1977 - Apple-II computer introduced.

1979 - Heathkit kicks off the HERO Robot Project.

1980 – Seymour Papert's Seminal book on Mindstorms; logo language.

1980 – Robotics Age Magazine kicks off, not addressing the industrial domain.

1981 - IBM pc computer introduced.

1982 - HERO Robots available..

1983 - RB5X introduced by RB Robot Corporation.

1984 - International Personal Robot Conference - Albuquerque.

1985 - International Personal Robot Conference - San Francisco

1987 - Beginning of the Robot Battles/Battlebots.

1990 – iRobot Corporation founded.

1997 – Honda's first autonomous humanoid robot, the P3.

1998 – Lego Mindstorm robotics modules introduced.

1999 – Sony's Aibo robot dog.

2003 – Robotshop founded.

2012 - Raspberry Pi board introduced

Drivers

What were the drivers for the development of personal robots? What stirred our imagination to implement these devices?

Star Wars

The first Star Wars movie by Lucas in 1977 set the bar high for robots. We were introduced to a humanoid robot, C-3PO, and a little maintenance 'droid, R2-D2. These worked! They did things, they interacted with people. It was there on the big screen. It could be done. The series of movies had a major impact on popular culture.

According to wikipedia, "R2-D2 was designed in artwork by Ralph McQuarrie and co-developed by John Stears but actually built by Tony Dyson, who ran his own studio called the *White Horse Toy Company* in the UK. Many scenes also made use of radio controlled and CGI versions of the character. Original props of R2-D2 and C-3PO are used as audio-animatronics in the queue area of Disneyland's Star Tours—The Adventures Continue attraction." Lucas acknowledges being influenced by the 3 robots in the earlier film *Silent Running*. "In the original *Star Wars* films, there were two R2-D2 models, one that was remote controlled and rolled on three wheeled legs, and another which was worn by English actor Kenny Baker and walked on two legs. There were a total of 15 R2-D2s on the set of *Attack of the Clones*. Eight were radio-controlled; two were worn by Baker; the remainder were stunt models that could be moved by puppet strings." What? Wait! They weren't computer controlled and autonomous? Next you'll tell me 3-CP0 was a puppet.

Reference:
http://www.starwars.com/databank/c-3po

Transformers

This popular Japanese series started in 1984. It was presented both on television and in comic books, and later as a series of movies and video games. The units were created in computer graphics. The whole Transformer ecosystem suggested what advanced robots could do. The spin-off video games and toys were quite popular. This seemed to suggest what advanced models were capable of. We obviously needed better computers.

Personal computers

The advent of the Apple-II and the IBM-pc brought computing to the masses. Nolan Bushnell (of Atari fame) called the resulting robots, "pc's on pc's." That's personal computers on push carts. The pc brought computing power down to a price an individual could afford. Size, weight, and power were problems, but there were clever solutions. There were extensive families of 8-bit microprocessors from Intel, Motorola, and others. These came in embedded computer format, meaning a single chip that had a cpu, some memory, and I/O. Embedded computing boards became available. An embedded computer is built into a system, such as a robot. They don't necessarily have to interface with a person via a keyboard and screen. They have a control function to do. They read sensors, and drive actuators. Programs for them could be developed on pc's. The pieces were coming together.

The Historical Units

This section discusses some of the more popular commercially available units from the unique period of personal robotic development in the 1980's. Literally, thousands of customized units came from the basements and garages of dedicated hobbyists. Some hobbyist and technology company's saw a large potential market, and Robot Stores, that at one time might have been Computer Stores or TV/Radio Stores, appeared.

Seymour's Papert's Logo language hid the complexity of programming. It was designed to teach grade school children to program. It allowed motion of an icon on a computer screen, called a turtle. Later, a small dome-shaped robot was connected by a wire, and was controlled by the program. It was a physical turtle. It was very simple, being controlled by the computer it was attached to. It had two driven wheels, and several bump switches. Interestingly, it had a pen in a solenoid holder. You could command "pen up" and "pen down". If you drove the robot around on a big piece of paper on the floor, it could write and draw – sort of a free ranging plotter.

Some of the company's survived the downturn of the Personal Robotics excitement, and some closed their doors. The level of excitement waned as the degree of difficulty was realized. The hobbyists focused their efforts into other areas, as the complexity of the problems became apparent. The problems were difficult, but not insurmountable.

The computers inside personal robots are classical embedded systems - they have limited user interface, usually do not host their own development systems, and are frequently called upon to handle real-time tasks. This has not prevented enthusiasts from using off-the-shelf pc hardware. This extends the limits of dedicated embedded controller boards, but does not necessarily address the real-time responsiveness requirement. This is mostly a operating system software issue. Standard linux, bsd, and Windows are NOT real-time operating systems. They are fast enough to appear to be, but will not correctly prioritize tasks in the real-time environment.

Embedded computer systems have certain unique characteristics. They support Real-Time requirements for tasks that have deadlines, or defined timing requirements for particular actions to be accomplished. They are event driven - the actions of the system are in response to events, not necessarily a predefined sequence. They are resource-constrained in terms of memory size, speed, power, weight, volume, interfaces, etc. And, they are special purpose - the device needs only to perform certain well defined tasks. This is opposed to the general purpose desktop, laptop, or tablet, which tries to do every task reasonably well.

The computers inside personal robot systems have gotten smarter by orders of magnitude since most of the units discussed here. Starting with 8-bit embedded controllers, we now have the luxury of using 64-bit multi-core cpu's with gigabytes of RAM memory and hundreds of gigabytes of external memory, all while using less power, taking up less space, and operating faster than the original units. And, incidentally, available at a very low cost. In addition, the support software is usually free with the hardware, and easy to use.

The Moore's law exponential increase in hardware capability has not been matched by a corresponding increase in software capability, or software development ease. This is true for off-the-shelf operating systems as well as the application software. A real-time system is defined as one in which the timing of the result is as important as the logical correctness. The right result at the wrong time is useless.

An operating system manages resources such as memory, I/O, interrupts, and tasks. It serves as the manager to arbitrates and enforces priorities. There are more than enough good operating systems, even with real-time support, to choose from. This is not suggesting that it is not worth while to write your own - you've got better things to do. However, you can't always plug in in and have it work as you hoped.

The early robots, the Hero series, the Gemini, RB5X, did not use operating systems per se. The functionality was there, buried in the code in a ROM, but it was mostly a state-based control loop with some interrupt capability. The application code was proprietary, and code interfaces were non-obvious.

Conferences

The International Personal Robotics Conferences were the result of the National Personal Robot Association (NPRA). Several conferences were held with enthusiastic hobbyists from around the world. The NPRA became the National Service Robot Association.

The first International Personal Robotics Conference was held in Albuquerque, New Mexico, in April of 1984. I attended with my family and my co-author on a presented paper, "Sensors for Robots, the Integration of Sensed Data, and Knowledge-Based Navigation Systems." The topic was in the area that would later be known as sensor fusion - taking different data from different sensors, and blending them together into a world view. We had been working with Heath's Hero-1, and the Gemini robot, from Arctec Systems. We used Polaroid ultrasonic rangefinder data, active infrared sensors, and optical sensors. Vision systems were in the future.

Albuquerque was the home of one of the early players of the personal computer revolution, MITS, whose 8-bit Altair computer kit sparked great interest. MITS, Micro Instrumentation and Telemetry Systems, was started as an electronics and telemetry company for Model Rocketry. By 1984, MITS was already history.

The show floor was a who's who of commercial firms and individuals involved in the emerging personal robot business. In retrospect, the technology base was not quite there yet. More than 25 years ago, personal robots was a high-interest, high-energy area, spurred on by the emergence of personal computers. Interest was high, due to the robots in the recently released Star Wars films.

The IPRC was the brainchild of Joe Bosworth, of the RB5X robot fame, and Nelson Winkless. The first IPRC had 500 seminar attendees and 3000 exhibit attendees.

The second International Personal Robotics Conference was held in San Francisco in 1985. I attended with my co-author with a paper entitled, ""Robot Hand Sensors for Object Location and Manipulation." We had done a lot of work with sensors mounted to the gripper of a HERO-1 robot, both tactile, and distance-sensing. There were a lot of new robotics products introduced since the previous years show. Momentum was building.

These shows and conferences were much different than the traditional Robot Shows, held in Detroit and Chicago, and featuring large hydraulic units weighing hundreds and thousands of pounds. The message was, you could build your own R2D2 for home use. Personal computers will enable this. It's a simple matter of software...

Heath Hero

In 1983, a robot for the home hobbyist with computer control was a significant item of technology. The development of this device was accomplished by Heath Company, of Benton Harbor, Michigan, producer of the popular Heathkits. In fact, the Hero Robot was available in both kit and assembled form.

The author bought one of these units at the local Heathkit store, complete with the arm, and began assembly immediately. Total construction stretched across some 2 weeks, with no major problems, due to Heath's extensive experience in kitting parts, and writing detailed and readable step-by-step manuals of exceptional clarity.

The main CPU was a Motorola 8-bit 6808, part of the 6800 series. The Motorola 6800 chip was introduced in 1975. It had a much simpler architecture than the Intel chips, with 72 instructions, and a single 16-bit index register. There were one to three bytes per instruction, The index register modifies operand addresses during execution, typically for vector/array operations. Before index registers and without indirect addressing, array operations were complicated to implement.

The 6800 was the first in a family of microprocessors and support chips. It had 8-bit wide data, and a 16-bit wide address bus. It required a single 5-volt power supply, and used a simple two-phase clock source. It was a synchronous design, so the clock could not be stopped or changed. It had a problem WAIT-ing for an external operation. A machine cycle was defined as a Phase 1 and a Phase 2 clock. During Phase1, the address for the instruction fetch was placed on the bus. During Phase 2, the instruction was read. On the next Phase 1, the instruction was executed. There were two sets of accumulators, A and B. All Input/Output was memory mapped; no separate I/O instructions were provided. The status register contained bits to indicate carry/borrow, overflow, zero, negative, and half-carry, as well as an interrupt mask.

All interrupts were vectored. The 6800 included a non-maskable interrupt (NMI). This fetched the contents from memory addresses FFFC and FFFD into the program counter, effectively forcing a jump to the contents of those addresses. The NMI was the highest priority interrupt. Interrupts were always serviced after the completion of the currently executing instruction. The normal interrupt

vectored through locations FFF8 and FFF9. The 6800 had a software interrupt instruction. Executing this instruction was just like
an external interrupt occurring. The difference was, it was synchronous to program execution. The program vectored through locations FFFA and FFFB. The RESET signal can be considered an interrupt. With a positive going edge on the reset line, program accessible registers were cleared, and hardware was initialized. The
interrupt mask bit was then set, locking out other interrupts. Then
the machine vectors through memory locations FFFE and FFFF.
There was also a WAIT instruction, that caused the processor to
stop processing and wait for a hardware interrupt.

Control signals were relatively simple. The VMA line indicated a
valid memory address on the address bus. The R/W signal indicated whether the bus was doing a read or write operation. BA indicated the bus was available, as the processor had tri-stated its data
and address bus and control lines. An Enable signal was available
from AND-ing Phase1 of the clock, and the VMA signal.

The HERO used the 6808 8-bit microprocessor, which was a 6800
pcu with 4 kilobytes of ram, and 8 kilobytes of rom. Offline storage was provided by a cassette interface. This used a standard audio cassette drive to store data expressed as tones at 300 baud. Better than nothing.

User input was accepted on a hex keypad, and output included six
hex LED's. More importantly, the voice synthesizer could be used
as output. One could get a memory dump read aloud, which helped
in debugging. The SC-01 speech synthesizer was a phoneme-based
unit. During initialization, the voice gave progress reports as
various systems were checked and verified. This is similar to the
BIOS function in pc's. A dictionary for the synthesizer was
provided. A remote control teaching pendant allowed guiding the

16

robot through a series of steps that were memorized, and could be repeated.

The drive was a dc motor, with a stepper motor for steering. The unit could move at three feet per second, and weighed 39 pounds. The shell measured 18x18 inches, and was 20 inches high.

The sensors included a Polaroid rangefinder, light and sound sensors digitized to 8 bits, and a motion detector. An optical encoder on a wheel provided an odometer function. There was a breadboard unit mounted on the head, with control and data signals brought out. This was ideal for prototyping.

The body had an aluminum structure, with molded plastic shells attached. The battery was a 12 volt, 4 amp-hour gelled lead acid unit. It was recharged manually using a plug-in charger. The head of the robot rotated 350 degrees, and carried most of the sensors and the arm.

The optional arm had 5 degrees of freedom, and could lift 16 ounces. It was controlled by software within the single 6808 processor. Stepper motors were used at each joint. The forearm assembly could extend and retract 5 inches. There was no elbow. The wrist could pivot up and down 90 degrees. It could also rotate 350 degrees. The hand was a two-fingered gripper, capable of opening about 3 ½ inches. There was no feedback in the arm. One interesting experiment was to coordinate wrist and shoulder angles, so the robot could lift a cup of water, without tilting and spilling it.

There was a single drive/steering wheel that was powered, and two idler wheels. With the weight on the driven wheel, it often diverged from its intended path, and didn't have anyway to tell. The wheel did have an odometer The steering mechanize was a stepper motor. For human interface, the head assembly had six 7-segment display, and a hex keypad. Keep in mind, with its voice synthesizer, the robot could talk to you. It also included a clock/calendar. There was a hand-held teaching pendant where your could operate the robot through a series of maneuvers, and it would store the sequence, and could repeat it.

Many high schools and colleges found the Hero unit to be ideal in an Introductory Robots course, and Heath provided the courseware.

Robots could share information, such as Asimov's book, their "bible."

Robots could water the plants.

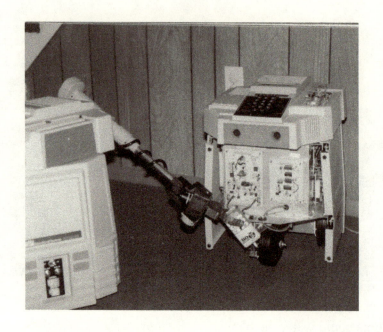

Robots could maintain other robots.

Robots could cook our meals.

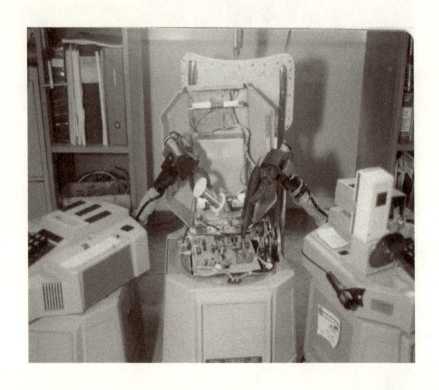

Most importantly, our robots could build more robots.

Upgrades

Software built into the Hero's computer would allow program loading and dumping in a serial format. This could be used with the cassette interface as described above, and could also be level shifted to RS-232 serial communications levels (-/+ 12 volts). This allowed a direct connection to a development computer, a pc that hosted 6800-family software tools.

One modification that was relatively easy to make was to add bi-aural hearing. The existing sound sensor was replaced by two small microphones on either side of the head, and an analog switch was used under program control to direct one of the two units to the existing analog to digital circuitry. A demonstration program would alternately sample the two inputs, and rotate the head until they were equal. When you spoke to the robot, it would politely turn to face you.

After the Y2K issue died down, I copied, modified, and burned a new PROM for the robot, which changed the year from "19" to "20". This allowed the spoken year to be correct. That took a pc connected to a PROM burner, and special software.

The Hero unit was a good ambassador. I was asked by a Public Relations firm to do a ribbon cutting ceremony for a new Federal facility. I modified a pair of scissors to fit the Hero's gripper, and determined the safest ribbon to cut would be a crepe-paper streamer. The day of the ceremony was a typical humid one in Washington, and as the ceremony droned on, the crepe paper got damper and damper, and sagged more and more. I had to keep nudging the support poles further apart to keep it taught. Finally, it was the robot's turn, and he did a little speech, and expertly cut the ribbon.

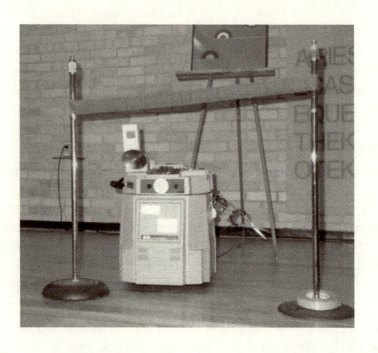

I did a similar ceremony for a local county library, which was attended by the county executive. Here, Hero and his scissors were accompanied by a Gemini robot. He got a round of applause, except from Gemini, who had no arms. My question, which was not answered, was whether a robot could get a library card?

I also accompanied the Hero when he did a television interview. The script was canned, and the anchorman only had to hit a key to get the next response. We practiced it, and it worked well. My role was to sit there and smile, as the anchor man and the robot discussed technology. As luck would have it in these situations, the software disappeared a few minutes from air time. We would have to type it back in manually, in hexidecimal. Turns out, anchorpersons are good readers with excellent diction. He read from the print-out, I typed, and the robot was ready in time. I sat there and smiled.

Hero-JR

The Hero was followed by a little brother, Hero-JR. The Junior did not have an arm, but the drive and steering were improved, and the computer was more capable. Plug-in cartridges, containing rom's, allowed for easy implementation of new features. The original Hero robot from Heath was quite a hit among hobbyists. The Junior model was less expensive. The head was fixed and did not rotate. It used a 12 volt, 4 amp-hour gell-cell lead acid battery, with a plug-in charger.

The unit had an embedded 6808 processor. I bought one of these units as a kit, and assembled it. The 6808 had 2 kilobytes of ram, expandable to 24 k, and a 32k ROM. It also had a RS-232 interface that can be used to communicate with the outside world. Shared memory between the 6808 and another processor was also possible. The existing system has a hex keypad and display, and a voice synthesizer. The most effective method of robot-to-human communication is with the voice unit. The sensor board also controls the robot drive and steering electronics.

The existing sensor suite included light and sound level sensors (digitized to 8 bits), a passive infrared motion detector, an active sonar ranging system, and the odometer. Actuators include the dc drive motor, and the steering motor. These are all interfaced to the CPU card via a custom I/O card in the robot.

Since the embedded 6808 processor already had a version of Wintek BASIC in ROM with all of the necessary robot-relevant constructs, that language was used. The existing embedded controller operated in closed-loop mode, commanding the motor

25

drivers and monitoring the odometer. It could also use the sonar and other sensors to detect impending collisions.

The Hero Basic language was contained in an 8-kbyte cartridge ROM. It allows for integers only, and the variables are A-Z. Control constructs are IF-THEN-ELSE, FOR-NEXT-STEP, GOTO, and GOSUB. Peek and Poke are supported, and (M6808) assembly language subroutines can be used. A useful command is the SPEAK "phoneme-list." The language could read the eye sensor (8 bits), sound sensor ("ear" 8 bits), the sonar rangefinder (1-157 inches), and a motion detector.

The 6808 was a classic 8-bit embedded processor with limited resources and human interface. I decided to upgrade the onboard computation resources with add-in units, under the constraint that the original computer system would not be touched. I also wanted to host the development environment for the 6808. This was enabled by the drop in cost and increase in capability of pc-based boards. The problem was the power draw.

Thirty years later, there have been major improvements in compute power and communications that the robot benefits from. The mobile robot platform is circa-1984. It operates from a rechargeable 12-volt battery, and has one driven steering wheel, and two idler wheels, one of which has an optical odometer. The computer had no secondary storage, and custom sensor and actuator interfaces. It has a simple hex keypad and display, and does include voice synthesis via an SC-01 chip. The robot draws 280 milliamps when it is not moving. In sleep mode, the robot wakes up briefly every 5 seconds or so to see if it should transition into operational mode. Sleep mode preserves the systems settings, while minimizing power draw. The system performs well with low-level servo tasks, but sorely needed a technology refresh. The existing electronics of the unit, although more than 25 years old, were working fine.

The primary design constraint was minimal modification of the robot system. This meant that added hardware had to operate from the 12-volt battery, and use existing interfaces to the embedded computer, not replace the existing embedded computer. This was partially due to lack of detailed documentation of the internals of the existing system, and partially the desire to preserve a classic system that was rapidly becoming a collectible. There are two electronics boards in the unit – one for sensor and motor interfacing, and the other for the CPU. Replacing the CPU card would entail re-programming the custom sensor and motor control. I made the decision to leave the existing electronics alone, and add a second computer board interfaced to the existing board via the RS-232 interface.

The desired modifications had several aspects: the new hardware, the new software, and the communications link.

Under the self-imposed constraint of minimum modification to the existing configuration, the added pc would connect to the existing embedded controller via its RS-232 serial line.

A variety of added Intel and Motorola-based computational platforms were tried. These were all either too limited in capability, or required too much power to operate. An IBM PS2/35 EX board drew 1.65-1.73 amps, with 4 megabytes of memory. A similar 386SX-40 board drew 1 amp with 4 megabytes of memory installed. A 68020 board drew about 1 amp. A Motorola 68HC11 board drew 110 ma, but had limited (8 kbytes) ram. It was hard to find an add-in CPU board that met the requirements and goals.

The Embedded Linux Journal (ELJ) Contest of 2001 provided me with a MZ-104 single chip pc computer board with embedded linux, in response to my proposed project entitled "LERP – Linux Embedded Robot Program".

The Linux Embedded Robot Project (LERP) was targeted to extending those resources and interfaces, and providing a development environment. The Linux-based MZ104 board was a pc-style architecture. All in all, the MZ014 board was ideal in this application, and provided processing, storage, and I/O resources that were not limiting. The low power MZ-104 was the answer.

The MZ-104 provided a single-chip PC-compatible computer capability, with a pc104-ISA bus. The configuration used is the MZ-104 motherboard, the 3-slot ISA expansion bus with a VGA card and 3Com 3C509 network interface card, and the system expansion board with serial, parallel, usb, keyboard, mouse, and game (A/D) ports. The CPU board supports a floppy drive and two standard IDE devices. It registers a blazing 38.4 -mips in performance. The MZ-104 board is pc-104 form factor (3.55 inch x 3.75 inch), and hosts an 8-megabyte disk-on chip device. The CPU board draws 0.6 amps at 5 volts.

The add-in CPU board can be used with a standard keyboard/mouse/VGA monitor, or can be remotely controlled from a networked (or inter-networked) computer running a remote desktop program. Thus the robot, as a node on the Internet, can be remotely controlled by any other computer on the Internet, and can relay to the master unit what it senses. This was Science Fiction when the Hero-Jr was designed and built.

The video card was an ISA bus unit, as this is what the MZ-104 expansion bus supports. This limits the capabilities of the video card. In fact, the video card did not supports the display mode required for a webcam, which requires a minimum resolution of 800 x 600 pixels, and 16 colors.

A power-switched floppy was included on the robot. It added minimal weight, and was normally powered off. A CD drive was added as needed to the ide interface. A DVD drive could be used as well.

The hard drive was a large power consumer. Standard hard drives in the 1-2 gigabyte range consumed about 5 watts. A laptop drive, which has the advantage of not requiring the 12-volt supply, draws about 1/2 of this, and is less shock sensitive as well. The ideal device, coming down in price rapidly, was the Compact Flash (CF) solid state card, adapted to emulate an ide drive. This consumes essentially no power and is non-volatile.

The hard drive allowed the MZ014 also to host the development environment for the 6808. This consists of a series of 6808 cross-software tools; an assembler, linker, and loader. It could also hold documentation in PDF form, and ROM maps.

These capabilities opened new world of opportunity; for example, it became trivial to interface a wireless NIC, a GPS unit, and video cameras (when appropriate devices drivers were available). When the wireless LAN was implemented, the keyboard and mouse, the VGA, and the hardwired LAN card became redundant except for low-level debugging. As the pc became part of a network, it was reachable by remote access from a convenient laptop. The onboard pc could also take advantage of large amounts of network-attached storage, off-platform computing power, and web-enabled applications.

There is a communications:storage trade-off with onboard resources. If something like a gps map database is required, it can either be stored onboard, or accessed over the wireless network connection from attached storage. The added computer provided a wireless interface to larger computers off of the platform. These network-based resources could be considered the "robot cloud."

The MZ014 was checked out with DOS and Windows, and with the BlueCat and ELKS Linux distributions. Since it was a standard pc-style architecture, interfacing with off-the-shelf hardware components was possible.

The robot was battery powered, so a custom power supply for the MZ104 was constructed. This uses a +12 volt input from the battery, and provided the necessary +12, -12 and +5 volts. Power consumption is a major issue for battery life. The MZ104 using serial console mode draws 500-560 ma. This rises to 890 ma with the floppy in use, and 1.78 amps with the hard drive in use. While the custom power supply was installed, a special jumper connection was added, to supplement the robot's 12 volt, 4 A-H battery. This allows an external 12 volt supply (such as a jump-start unit for a car) to be used to run the robot on the bench, and charge the battery. This is in addition to the robot's small wall-mount recharger.

The embedded 6808 processor board was connected to the MZ104 via an asynchronous serial line, using a 9600E71 protocol. When the 6808 is running its built-in BASIC interpreter (in cartridge-ROM), the MZ104 acts as a terminal, to download BASIC programs to the 6808 (the alternative being 6800 assembly language). LOGO would be a better choice, but it is not ported to the 6808. Logo can be run under Linux or Windows, on the MZ104.

The MZ014 computer was built into the base of the robot, and powered from the battery. The floppy and hard drive were included, but not normally powered. The serial console of the MZ104 is tied to a development LINUX box.

The LOGO programming language is used to direct the robot's activities. The LOGO system acts as a "just-in-time" production facility for code the embedded controller understands, which is downloaded over the RS-232 line, and executed.

This was an interesting augmentation project, taking place over a period of 6 years. In the LERP project, the MZ104 hosts the development environment and provided high-level guidance to an existing embedded MC6808 device controller within the robot. The Linux-based processor was to run higher-order packages based on Logo, Java, Python, or other languages, while the 6808 board is limited to assembler or BASIC. At this time, I found Logo to be the right solution.

But, as time went on, there was an even better solution than the MZ-104. An embedded pc was added with minimal modification. The embedded pc brings modern interfaces and capabilities such as wireless LAN, usb connections, sufficient memory for advanced language support, and secondary memory devices such as hard drives and CD/DVD drives. The selected board was a mini_ITX pc motherboard, using the Intel Atom processor operating at 1.6 GHz. It has 1 gigabyte of RAM, serial and parallel interfaces, four usb ports, a LAN connection, and built-in video and sound. I added a 20 gigabyte laptop (2.5") IDE disk drive. I installed Windows-XP, a Zonet usb w-lan, and a usb camera. A CD or DVD can be connected via the USB for software loading. The only interface the board lacks is the game (or joystick) board, which can also be used as a dual channel A/D. This is easily added with a USB adapter. The total cost of the CPU board plus memory was $60. Windows-XP was chosen because the version of LOGO that runs under this operating system has I/O support. The XP footprint can be minimized, and no hard real time tasks are require of it. The board brings with it the ubiquitous USB interface, which allows for the seamless integration of devices such as gps and webcams.

The added processor operates from the robot's +12 volt battery. The power supply is a marvel of miniaturization, being built entirely on the ATX power supply mating connector. It is an 80-watt unit, supplying the voltages that the motherboard and disks require. On the bench, a standard wall-power supply can be substituted to conserve the battery. The added CPU card drew 1.85 amps with the laptop hard drive. A CF flash- based hard drive does not significantly reduce the power draw.

Architectural models of Hierarchical control

The robot's embedded computer acts as the lowest level of control, the servo level, interfacing with sensors and actuators. The added pc acts as an intermediate level of control. Additional computational resources can provide higher levels of goal-seeking control to the system via a wireless connection. This follows the general principals of the NASREM model, based on work at NIST and NASA, and the Flight Telerobotic Servicer Project.

The existing 6808 board hosts the servo level control, providing a closed-loop with the motor and sensors, and receiving commands from the next higher level. This corresponds to Arkin's (see references) reflective or reactive level, and the cortex level is more like Arkin's deliberative level of control. This next higher level is the supervisory level, which decides what to do. Above that level, and implemented external to the platform, is the world model.

The Logo system running on the pc board presents an abstraction layer between the user and the underlying hardware at the servo level. The details of the servo level are hidden. The user does not operate at the "brain stem" level, but at the "cortex" level with goals and schema, not control and status bits.

Added Software

The pc board was checked out with Windows and various linux distributions such as RedHat 6.2, BlueCat 3.0, and the ELKS. Linux is the ideal operating environment for the added computer system. With Linux, you can control the software components in the system build. In this particular application, the computer does no "real-time" processing. A very simple, streamlined Linux, the VectorLinux distribution, was finally chosen. This distribution works well with limited resources. The installed version was 4.3. It is supposed to require a minimum Pentium-166, but was happy on the Pentium-100 equivalent of the MZ-104 board. The unpacking of install packages did take a while. Eventually, I loaded the software on another, faster system, and then moved the hard drive. VectorLinux will run in 32 megabytes of memory, and a minimum load has an 850-megabyte footprint on the hard drive.

VectorLinux used kernel 2.6.7 The size of the load can be kept under 1 gigabyte, allowing the use of a CF card in place of a hard drive. LILO was not completely happy with the CF card, so GRUB was substituted.

Logo is the ideal language in which to program robots. It is designed by Seymour Papert for small children to do just that. It is derived from Lisp (but has fewer parentheses). It has very simple concepts and constructs to allow users to use the language rapidly to achieve immediate results. Python is sometimes referred to as the "new Logo" but lacks the turtle graphics. Berkeley logo (UCBlogo) is available for Linux platforms. The tested version was 5.4. MSWlogo, based on Berkeley, is reported to run under WINE.

Consider a Logo program to move a robot in a square; we will refer to this procedure as "squaredance." The program consists of a linear movement followed by a 90-degree turn, repeated 4 times. In Hero Basic, this would be accomplished by 4 executions of the program:

FWD 1

RT 90

The equivalent Logo would be:

to squaredance

repeat 4 [fd 1 rt 90]

end

This commands the turtle, the onscreen graphics object, to execute the motion. What remains is to translate the motion commands from logo to basic, and to communicate these to the robot via the RS-232 interface. The computers are connected with a short serial null-modem cable, a 25 pin connector on the robots side, and a 9-pin connector on the pc side.

Here are the correspondences in Hero-BASIC and Logo for the motion primitives:

HeroBasic	Logo
FWD inches	FD x
BWD inches	BACK x
Left deg	LT deg
Right deg	RT deg

The serial port must be opened and configured:

Portopen "com1

Portmode "com1:9600,e,7,1

At the end, we would normally close the port:

portclose

Metaprogramming

Metaprogramming refers to the production of programs for other computers. In this case, the LOGO program synthesizes a BASIC program from templates, and stores it as a list. A metaprogram is a program that produces code, much like a compiler. If we produce code for a different architecture, we have a cross-compiler. This process is implemented on the robot in near-real time.

Logo procedure to Move Forward

```
to Moveforward
    fd 3                            ; move the turtle object on
the screen
    portopen "com1
    portmode "com1:9600,e,7,1
    show portwritechar 13           ; send a character
return, check response
    show portread char
    make "buff {70 87 68 32 49 13} ; synthesize a list that says
"FWD 3 <cr>
    show portwritearray 6 :buff     ; output the list of 6
characters
    portclose
    end
```

The latest for Hero Jr., now 30 years old, is yet another update involving the Raspberry Pi architecture. An evolution from the pc, the Pi provides a linux-based deck-of-cards sized processor. Running linux, any number of applications, such as a web server (Apache) are available.

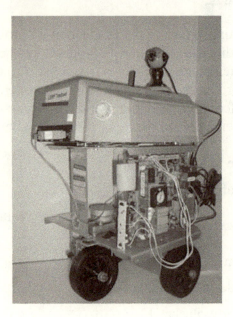

Newer Options

Emerging architectures allow us to put 32-bit processors to augment the robot's capabilities.

The Raspberry Pi is a small, inexpensive, single board computer based on the ARM architecture. It is targeted to the academic market. It uses the Broadcom BCM2835 system-on-a-chip, which has a 700 MHz ARM processor, a video GPU, and currently 512 M of RAM. It uses an SD card for storage. The Raspberry Pi runs the GNU/linux and FreeBSD operating systems. It was first sold in February 2012. Sales reached ½ million units by the Fall. Due to the open source nature of the software, Raspberry Pi applications and drivers can be downloaded from various sites. It requires a single power supply, and dissipates less than 5 watts. It has USB ports, and an Ethernet controller. It does not have a real-time clock, but one can easily be added. It outputs video in HDMI resolution, and supports audio output. I/O includes 8 general purpose I/O lines, UART, I2C bus, and SPI bus.

The Raspberry Pi design belongs to the Raspberry Pi Foundation in the UK, which was formed to promote the study of Computer Science. The Raspberry Pi is seen as the successor to the original BBC Microcomputer by Acorn, which resulted in the ARM processor.

Using the LAMP (Linux-Apache-MySql-PHP) approach, Web enabled applications running on the robot, such as a remotely accessed parameter page, and web cam are now easy. The robot is able to measure and report its battery voltage and the ambient temperature. We can add tilt sensors, an electronic compass, and GPS. The processor is powerful enough to handle a video camera or two.

Most of the robot's interaction (robot-to-person) is centered on the built-in speech synthesizer. An interesting feature is the spoken progress of the self-test and calibration routine. In the robot's BASIC interpreter, the system can say a phrase, enclosed in parenthesis. Since the Pi can host a Siri type ap, voice command and interaction is feasible. Berkeley Logo is available for Linux.

Future Directions

Emerging standards, such as those proposed by the Robotic Engineering Task Force, will help to ensure that, in the future, control algorithms and programs, as well as the hardware itself, will be common across robotic platforms. For example, an "explore" program should not care whether the underlying hardware is wheeled, tracked, buoyant, or winged. The application of Open source hardware and software accelerates the spread of applications across the research community.

We can envision swarms of cooperating mobile robot platforms, deployed for a variety of purposes in hazardous environments. Modeled on the behavior patterns of insects, these groups of robots will act individually according to local conditions, but in cooperation with their peers, without a "master plan" or top-down control. StarLogo, from the MIT Media Lab, implements multiple interacting turtles, leading to implementation of robot teams and swarms. A distributed StarLogo, implemented in software agents, provides the basis for multiple cooperating robots.

The robot's embedded computer acts as the lowest level of control, the servo level, interfacing with sensors and actuators. The added pc acts as an intermediate level of control. Additional computational resources can provide higher levels of goal-seeking control to the system via the wireless connection. These resources can now be cloud based. This unit is still in operation at this writing.

Hero-2000

The Hero-2000 robot was vastly superior to either of the predecessor units. In fact, Heath assembled a panel of experts at the factory to evaluate a pre-production model, and its advances were readily apparent. It used a 16-bit processor with a modular bus structure, and a series of 8-bit controllers dedicated to servo and sensor tasks. The computer could interface with a disk drive and utilized a bus structure. Although not DOS-compatible, the system was very close. The next unit would most certainly use a standard pc architecture.

A lot of robot enthusiasts adopted the Hero Robot from Heathkit, and extended its capabilities with new hardware and software. When Heath developed a new generation robot, the Hero-2000, they selected a cross-section of early adopters to come out to the Benton Harbor plant, and critique the Hero-2000 (ET-19) before it was introduced. I was one of the lucky few, based on my relationship with the Heath robot folks.

The Hero-2000 robot was vastly superior to either of its predecessor units. The main 16-bit cpu had I/O port communication windows with 9 servo level controllers, which were 8-bit dedicated systems handling control axis in the arm and base such as wrist, elbow, and shoulder. A remote link and keyboard was provided. Sensors included 360 degree coverage sonar, with light, temperature, and sound sensing. The charger was an auto-dock, that the robot could seek and find when the batteries got low.

The main processor was a 16-bit Intel 8088, with 8-bit Intel 8042 units as slaves, 6 in the main configuration, with 5 more in the arm, one for each joint. This allowed each joint to be moved simultaneously, something the original Hero could not do. The arm had a gripper with a sense of touch, and could lift a pound. The main CPU had 24 kilobytes of ram, expandable to 576. It had a 64k ROM with BASIC.

The Intel 8088 CPU was a variant of the Intel 8086 and was introduced on July 1, 1979. It had an 8-bit external data bus instead of the 16-bit bus of the 8086. The 16-bit registers and the one megabyte address range were the same The original IBM PC was based on the 8088 chip.

The Intel 8042 was an 8-bit embedded controller. It has a modified Harvard Architecture with internal (2k x 8) or external program ROM and 256 bytes of internal RAM. The I/O is mapped into its own address space, separate from programs and data. It has a memory efficient one-byte instruction set, and mature development tools. The 8042 is also used in the IBM AT keyboard.

The Hero-2000 used a new bus-based architecture based on Heath's PC-compatible computers. It was similar to the S-100 bus in timing and signal definitions, but used different connectors. The cards were 5" x 11", compared to AT standard cards of 4" x 13". The connector was totally different, being a unique 72-pin configuration. The bus provided 12 card slots. Prototyping was relatively easy to do. The next generation of the system would most certainly have used a standard pc bus architecture, and evolved into a Windows-based system. The H-2000 used a customized version of MS-DOS.

Two RS-232 ports were provided with, again, cassette-based storage. A 5 1/4 inch floppy was available, but was both heavy and power-hungry.

We marveled at how far the architecture had advanced from the Hero-1 model (and the Hero-Jr), and praised the open architecture, allowing new hardware and software to be developed. The H-2000 was a pricey unit, and sales would never justify the development expense. In fact, Heath would not last too much longer as an electronics kit manufacturer, as the new breed of experimenter was not into that aspect of the hobby.

The development of the hardware and software was only one aspect of a Heath design. The dummy-proof instructions for assembly needed to be developed and tested, and a series of debugging and test procedures were required. The parts had to be kitted and packaged. For any one who ever built a Heathkit, the effort that went into the little details behind the scenes was apparent.

I regret never having purchased the 2000 model. I did do some design work with add-in hardware, and used a friend's model for testing around 1992. The integrated circuits in the H-2000 were standard NMOS parts, and could be replaced with their more costly CMOS equivalents for reduced power consumption. For example, the 8088 CPU running at 5 MHz could be replaced with the V20 processor equivalent. Similar swap-outs were possible with the support chips such as the interrupt controllers.

With stars in our eyes, we went back home to await the units being available in our local Heathkit stores. We had seen what could be done in the future. The Hero-2000 is a formidable unit, even today.

Heathkit tried to reenter the educational robot business in 2007. The HE-ROBOT incorporates an onboard computer running Windows XP Professional on a Core 2 Duo Processor. It was 21 inches tall, weighed 55 pounds, and had a 80 Gigabyte hard drive. It included IR sensors, bright LED headlights, and space for custom project circuitry. It never appeared on the market, in spite of being a very impressive unit.

Gemini

The Gemini Robot, by Arctec Systems of Columbia, Maryland, was one of the more advanced designs of the time. The Gemini robot was built on the smart mobile base. This was a 4-wheeled system, with one wheel on each side driven, and the other wheel slaved via a belt. There were two dc motors, with optical encoders, and a closed loop servo control based on the 6502 chip. The smart mobile base received high-level commands from the main robot controller such as move forward or backward so many units or turn so many degrees. The robot design was based on multiple 6502 8-

bit processors, the same as used in the Apple-II. At the time, the IBM pc was not yet available, and would prove to be more expensive than the Apple-II system. Also, the Apple-II architecture was expandable, with a bus architecture. It was not the fastest or most inexpensive, but it was the technology of choice at the time.

Introduced in 1975, the MOS Technologies 6502 became famous as the engine of the Apple computer. It operated at 1 MHz, and used 4,000 transistors in NMOS technology. It operated from a single 5 volt supply. The earlier 6501 was pin-compatible with Motorola's 6800, not software compatible, but ran into legal problems. Variations included the 6510 with added I/O ports, the 6507 with a reduced 13-bit address bus. The chip was also produced in CMOS technology. It was also used in the Atari and Commodore computers.

The 6522 dual 8-bit parallel port and dual timer chip supported the CPU. The 6502 could also use 6800 peripherals. It allowed for indirect addressing, which neither the 8080 or the 6800 had.

As opposed to most of the other 8-bit CPU designs, the 6502 was little endian. It was limited in registers, having one data register, two index registers, and a stack pointer. It used a PLA for instruction decode and sequencing. Like most microprocessor of the times, the 6502 had undocumented instructions, certain bit patterns that would do strange things. In the 6502's case, the JAM instruction would cause the CPU to freeze, requiring a hard reset. The 6502 remains a popular architecture, and 16 bit and CMOS variations were developed. It was second-sourced by GTE, Rockwell, and NCR. At the time, the same architecture implemented by different manufacturers had different behavior for the same undocumented instructions. This was exciting, but limited code portability. Gemini could also do an autodock with its charger.

43

RB5X

The RB5X^{tm} robot was introduced by the RB Robot Corporation of Golden, Colorado in 1983, preceding Heath's popular Hero robot to market by a few months. It was microprocessor controlled, and included a serial interface for connection to an external computer or terminal. It has a charger docking connector on its lower body. The body was cylindrical, 23 inches high with a 13 inch diameter polycarbonate dome. It weighed 24 pounds, a tight and attractive design. There are two 4-inch diameter drive wheels, and 2 casters. The RB5X design is attributed to Joe Bosworth, a founder of the National Personal Robot Association. Joe was associated with Smartrobots.com, with a new unit similar in appearance to the RB, but with much more capability.

The RB's computer, a National Semiconductor 8073 8-bit CPU, was programmed in National's TinyBasic language. The 8070-series cpu's had onboard ram and ROM, 8-bit wide data, and a 16-bit wide address bus. They included hardware multiply and divide, and operated from a single +5 volt supply. The nominal memory was 8 kilobytes, with 16 kilobytes additional as an option, using 6116 dram chips. The processor could address a total of 64k bytes of memory, and the TinyBasic interpreter took up only 2.5 bytes. SAVVY was developed to be a conversational control language for the RB5X. RCL, the Robot Control Language, was available for the Apple-II or IBM PC platforms. Three INS8255 triple 8-bit parallel ports were included for I/O. A radio link was developed to eliminate the RS-232 cable.

Eight bumpers along the lower body were tied directly to a CPU-readable register. A second register's control bits enabled the sonar, the infrared LED, various other LED's and a horn. A third 8-bit register controlled the two motors via relays, and inputted the battery voltage, the charger sense, and the sonar return pulse. The robot sensed its charger via reflected IR at the base. The robot could also follow a line on the floor, which was in a contrasting color.

Two batteries were used with the unit, both being sealed lead-acid. One handled the electronics, and a larger one powered the drive motors and other higher current loads.

The RB5X had an optional arm assembly, with its own controller electronics. A manual control box was included, and the arm was also controlled via software. There were shoulder, elbow and wrist joints, and a gripper.

A voice module was also available as an option. This used the SC-01 phoneme synthesis voice chip, and a General Instruments AY-3-8910 Programmable Sound Generator.

The RB5X found early acceptance in the K-12 education community, both because it was appealing to the kids, and was easy to use. A fair amount of courseware was developed, and studies were done of the effectiveness of RB5X as a teaching tool.

The RB5X was quite a hit in the education market. It wais still available for a while, but rather pricey at $3,495 for the basic unit. It stared on the TechTV series, a show aired on May 3, 2002. There is a Yahoo discussion group on the RB5X, and numerous units may still be found in schools and with robot enthusiasts and historians.

The company is still around, http://www.rbrobotics.com/

Topo-Bob

The T.O.P.O robot, also called BoB was produced by Androbot, Inc., was a concept of Nolan Bushnell of Atari fame. B.o.B stood for Brains on Board, a reference to the onboard microprocessor. Designed in the 1980's, it was targeted to the consumer and educational markets. It's development system was an Apple-II or a Windows-95/98 computer. It had its own programming languages (Apple-II BASIC, Logo, or Forth), but suffered from the lack of sensors. It entered the market in 1983. T.O.P.O was constructed of molded plastic with 2 drive wheels, and stood 36" tall. Arms on Topo 1 and 2 would fold out, but there were no hands or grippers. Topo 3 didn't have an arm..

Topo used three of the Intel 8031 embedded 8-bit processors. This was a rom-less version of the popular 8051. This was a single chip cpu with memory and I/O. They had serial I/O plus dual timers, 4k of ROM, and 128 bytes of RAM. They operated up to 16 MHz,

Communication was via a radio or infrared transmitter attached to a personal computer. Topo 2 and 3 used an infrared transmitter, and could be controlled by a four-way pad on the top of their head that also served as the infrared receiver.

In its final versions, Topo included a text-to-speech processor, so that users could program their robots to speak. A fourth model was made but it never went into production It was more like the BoB (Brains On Board, a unreleased robot that was produced after the Topo series) robot than a Topo.

Another member of the Androbot family was the F.R.E.D., the Friendly Robot Educational Device, a short, squat robot only 12 inches high. Like the original Terrapin Turtle (designed for Logo), Fred had a pencil. He also had a voice synthesizer with a 45 word vocabulary. He could act as a fairly elaborate plotter, moving around a large sheet of paper. FRED cost $350 in 1983.

Battlebots

BattleBots was an offshoot of the original American version of *Robot Wars*, a British game show modeled on a US-based competition of the same name. It was broadcast on BBC Two from 1997 until 2003, with its final series in 2003 and 2004. In 2003, the enthusiasts themselves formed The Fighting Robot Association and with their associated event organizers, carry on participating in competitions for new audiences.

The series involved teams of amateur and professional robot builders who made their own robots to fight against each other in both friendly and tournament matches. As well as fighting each other, they had to avoid the "House Robots", which were not bound by the same weight or weapon limits as the contestants. It should be noted that the robots in these instances are directly radio-controlled, and are best described as tele-robots.

BattleBots is an American company that hosts robot competitions. BattleBots is also the name of the television show created from the competition footage. BattleBots Inc. is headquartered in Vallejo, California and holds most of its competitions in San Francisco. In a BattleBots event the competitors are remote-controlled armed and armored machines, designed to fight in an arena combat elimination tournament. If both combat robots are still operational at the end of the match the winner is determined by a point system based on damage, aggression, and strategy. The first season of Battlebots aired in August 2000.

The Battlebots events had a loyal following, but had its final episode in 2011.

PDA-based robotics

Personal Digital Assistants (PDA's) such as the Palm Pilot had enough computational capability to handle small, well-defined robot tasks. They had the advantage of being low-power and moderately low-cost, but lacked many of the standard interfaces. They did have built-in communication capability, and this made them ideal for swarms of co-operating mini-robots. The limited input-output capability of PDA's made them less than ideal platforms for robots, but their modern replacements, tablet computers can sometimes be used on robot platforms.

Evolutionary Approaches

This section discusses some follow-on approaches to robot platforms for personal use.

Lego Mindstorms

The Lego Group provides a line of programmable robotics components, including motors, sensors, cables, mechanical parts, software, and controllers. These were introduced in 1998, and have been continually updated.

The Mindstorm kits are marketed as an educational tool, with a partnership with MIT Media Lab. The ROBOLAB software was developed at Tufts University, and is based on the National Instruments LabView software. Standard programming languages such as c, c++, Forth, Visual Basic, and Java can also be used.

The first generation Mindstorms used a 8-bit controller, the Robotic Command Explorer (RCX), based on the Hitachi H8. It had 32 kilobytes of memory. A Mac or pc can be used as the development computer, and the interface link is infrared. The NXT units use an ARM-7 cpu. Multiple RCX units can communicate and interact. Each has three sensor input ports and three more output ports. It is designed for battery power.

A USB webcam is also available. This is used with the Vision Command software, which runs basic detection algorithms.

The Mindstorms NXT model of 2006 has three servo motors and sensors for sound, light, touch, and an ultrasonic ranger. Bluetooth short-range radio is also available. NXT-2, in 2009, featured a color sensor, and the controller supports floating point operations.

VEX

The Vex systems is a family of robotics parts including sensors, structure, motors, mobility systems such as wheels and treads, and controllers. World-wide competitions are held for robots using the

Vex kits. The first was in 2005. Vex robotics is heavily into the classroom market.

Roomba

The Roomba is an autonomous robotic vacuum cleaner sold by iRobot. Under normal operating conditions, it is able to navigate a living space and its obstacles while vacuuming the floor. The Roomba was introduced in 2002; as of January 2008, iRobot claims that over 2.5 million units have been sold. Several updates and new models have since been released that allow the Roomba to better negotiate obstacles and optimize cleaning.

More interesting, the Roomba is sold without the vacuuming part. This provides a low-cost robotics platform. The interfaces to the build-in controller are easily accessed. An ARM-7 processor is used for control.

Roombas come with a Mini-DIN connector supporting a TTL serial interface; third-party adapters are available to access the Roomba's computer via Bluetooth, USB, or RS-232 (PC/Mac serial). The Roomba Open Interface (formerly "Roomba Serial Command Interface") API allows programmers and roboticists to create their own enhancements to Roomba. Several projects are described on Roomba hacking sites.

In response to this interest, the company manufactures the iRobot Create, with the vacuum cleaner motor replaced by a "cargo bay" for mounting devices like TV cameras, lasers, and even otherwise non-mobile robots. The Create provides a greatly enhanced, 25-pin interface providing both analog and digital bidirectional communication with the hosted device. It can then be used as the mobile base and wireless interface for completely new robots.

Robosapien

Robosapien, introduced in 2004, is a popular anthropomorphic robot toy with advanced features. It has arms and grippers, and could actually throw objects. It had a voice unit as well. Supposedly, over 1.5 million units were sold.

At the German Open 2005 tournament two teams of three RoboSapiens played the first Soccer match of humanoid robots worldwide. A pda was included in the robot for the vision system. An advanced version, the Robosapien X can be controlled by an Apple tablet.

The robot has a loyal following and active development community.

Reference:
http://www.robocommunity.com

Enabling Technology

The deployment of Personal robots is enabled by rapid advances in technology. These include enhanced computational and communication capabilities, new materials, new power sources, and the commoditization of advanced technology. Moore's law continues to enhance the capability of the technology, while simultaneously lowering the price. Building-block modules of increasing complexity can be used at the college, high school, and elementary level.

Smart Sensors, and Sensornets

Smart sensors include embedded processing. The IEEE Standard 1451 covers functions, communication protocols, and formats for smart sensors. Networked and wireless sensors are also covered. Moving the processing closer to the sensor offloads this task from the main computer, freeing up resources for other tasks. Sensor fusion is also applicable. This is the merging of inputs from different sensor types to achieve a better knowledge of a situation or event.

A group of sensors working together can be organized into a network. These can be an array of similar or identical sensors, or a group of sensors using different technologies to gather a more complete perspective of the sensed item of interest. The sensor network can be wired or wireless. The detection devices monitor the local conditions and perform a small local area surveillance, collect data, and translate the acquired raw data to usable information. The network can be rigidly preplanned, or ad-hoc and self-organizing. This latter approach involves swarms of sensors, not all of which need to be the same.

Sensornets are groups of autonomous (smart) sensors, distributed over a certain space. They are connected in a node-network architecture. The system can be wired, but is usually wireless, for convenience. Sensor nets have been used, for example, to monitor forest fires, and water quality. These little sensor systems have to be inexpensive, and have low power consumption. Loss of individual nodes does not greatly impact the system. A mobile robot platform might be a node on a sensor-net.

Internet, and IoT

The Internet of Things is built upon web-accessible embedded systems. More and more embedded systems are on the web. This allows to integrate cheap embedded devices with ubiquitous web services, accessible with wireless technologies. An example might be smart electric meters. Smart devices, including rovers, can access data, provide data, or access services.

To make use of this concept, we need uniquely identifiable objects such as smart sensors, smart actuators, smart platforms. What is the identity scheme? The Uniform Resource Locater (URL) approach can be adopted We also need advanced connectivity to the Internet, which provides distance-insensitive world-wide connectivity. These are large areas of the Earth's surface where the Internet does not reach, but satellite links can be used, although this is an expensive approach. The polar regions enjoy good satellite communications due to a series of polar orbiting spacecraft.

This whole thing is just getting started as of 2014. There may now be more "things" on the Internet than people. There is a huge ecosystem of devices, talking to cloud servers, and among themselves. This reduce the reliance on people (who needs us anyway?).

Cloud servers allow access to "unlimited" datasets and resources. The latest trend is cloud robotics, where a connected mobile platform can offload computational and storage resources by having a good communications link.

The connectivity is enabled by the .net framework, which is open source. This allows the embedded device to be a http client. The .net framework supports most of the embedded computational architectures, including the popular Arduino.

Very-low-cost, high-performance microprocessor-based embedded systems enable wide applications. Most of these boards, complete 32-bit computers with memory and I/O cost
less than $50. Add-on boards provide GPS location finding, wifi and bluetooth connectivity, 3-axis gyros, etc.

Free and open source software and collaborative development environments enhance the deployment process. There are standard software interfaces for communication protocols.

Mobile platforms

An increasing number of off-the-shelf inexpensive platforms allow the person robot builder to focus on the electronics and software. These platforms are tracked or wheeled, they float or submerge, or can hover or fly. Many radio-controlled models, boats, submersibles, electric aircraft, cars, and trucks are readily available and inexpensive. These serve as the mobility platforms for integrating computational, sensor, and communication packages.

Interfacing the motors and actuators of the various devices to the onboard computer is relatively simple. The computer works with low voltages and currents, and provides control signals. We need a motor driver (chip, board) to provide the power to the motors. Generally, the computer controller has to provide a direction bit (forward, backward), and a pulse-width modulation (pwm) signal that sets speed. That's for dc motors. There are also servo actuators. AC motors are generally not found on mobile robots, because the onboard power source is dc batteries. You can convert, but there is an efficiency issue.

Pulse width modulation control is typically used for motor speed control. In this scheme, the width of a pulse determines the duty cycle of the motor, from 0 to 100%. The pulse repetition rate must be greater than the motor's inertia will allow it to see. Typically, this works well with 1 kilohertz, although systems up to 100 KHz are used. During the period of time when the pulse is not active, the back-emf (electro-magnetic force) of the motor can be measured as an indicator of load, and the next pulse adjusted accordingly.

Today, small servo systems developed for model aircraft and cars are cheap and plentiful. These normally use radio links as a control mechanism. The system consists of an electric motor and a variable resistor for position feedback. The radio link sends a PWM signal, where the width of the pulse indicates a position command. The feedback allows the servo to hold the commanded point. The standard servos used in radio controlled models use a 50-Hertz frame rate. Each pulse has a 20-millisecond width.

The actual mechanism may be capable of 90, 180, or possibly 360-degree rotation. The system was originally developed as analog (continuous), but is now digital (discrete). Interfaces between servo systems and standard computer interfaces such as USB are available.

Solenoids are linear motion devices using a coil and magnet. They are used for actuating valves, for example. They require a simple application of voltage for operation. Working against a spring, a fairly accurate position can be maintained, at the cost of continuously applied current.

Feedback from an actuator to the control computer can be provided by a sensor. For example, a odometer measures the distance the driven wheel has turned. The sensor-controller-actuator loop is essential for correct control

Advanced Battery technology

Batteries have gotten better, due to new applications in hybrid and full-electric cars, small electric aircraft and boats, and cell phones.

Rechargeable batteries in new chemistries are also the outgrowth of hybrid and full electric vehicles. The energy density is very high. Technologies like lithium-polymer (LioP) have created expanded the operating life of equipment before recharging is required, and allowed for solar recharge. These types of batteries were used in consumer electronics by 1995.

They also have the advantage of being lightweight, and they also provide a higher discharge rate (greater current) than other battery technologies. However, overcharge, over- discharge, and penetration can result in explosion. Special charging circuits are required, as well as temperature and discharge current monitoring.

It is relatively simple to monitor the battery voltage and current. You can integrate the current to get the energy usage, and tell when the battery needs recharging. It can also give you an indication of a stuck mechanism.

Don't let me scare you when I say "integrate." No calculus needed. Just add up the current measured for a period of time. Temperature of the battery pack is also sometimes a concern. Check to see if the battery is exothermic (gives off heat; gets hot) when it is charged or discharged. In one case, where we were working on a Greenland robot, we had to keep the batteries from freezing with the waste heat from the computer.

Embedded processors

Advances driven by cellular phones and data systems have made available small powerful processors that rival a datacenter of a few years back. They are designed for communication, and include a variety of interfaces. The devices are multicore, meaning there is more than one cpu. They can include specialty cores such as floating point or digital signal processing. They have memory integrated with the cpu. They support analog as well as digital interfaces. The boards tend to be deck-of-cards size or smaller, and typically cost under $50. Some examples include Arduino, Maple, Raspberry Pi, and Beaglebone..

This section presents and discusses some "real-world" embedded systems, at both the chip and system-level, that can be applied for robots.

Arduino

The Arduino is a simple open-source single-board microcontroller. The hardware consists of a simple open hardware design for the Arduino board with an Atmel processor and on-board I/O support. The software support includes a standard compiler and a boot loader that runs on the board, along with numerous libraries of code.

Arduino hardware is programmed using a language similar to C++ with some simplifications and modifications, and an IDE.

The project began in Italy in 2005 to produce a device for implementing student-built design projects less expensively. By mid-2011, more than 300,000 Arduino boards had been shipped.

An Arduino board consists of an 8-bit Atmel AVR microcontroller or an Atmel 32-bit ARM. An important aspect of the Arduino is the standard way that connectors are arranged, allowing the CPU board to be connected to a variety of interchangeable add-on modules called *shields*. Shields allow for interfacing with sensors and actuators, as well as general I/O. Most boards include a 5-volt linear regulator and a 16 MHz crystal oscillator although some designs dispense with the on-board voltage regulator. An Arduino's microcontroller comes with a boot loader that simplifies uploading of programs to the on-chip flash memory.

Boards are programmed over an RS-232 serial connection. Serial Arduino boards contain a simple inverter circuit to convert between RS-232-level and TTL-level signals. Newer Arduino boards are programmed via serial communications over USB.

The Arduino board brings out the microcontroller's I/O pins for use by external circuits.

The Arduino IDE is a cross-platform application implemented in Java. It is designed to introduce programming to newcomers unfamiliar with traditional software development. It includes a code editor with features such as syntax highlighting, parenthesis matching, automatic indentation, and is also capable of compiling and uploading programs to the board with a single click. There is generally no need to edit makefiles or run programs on the command line.

The Arduino IDE comes with a C/C++ library called "Wiring", which makes many common input/output operations much easier. It uses the gnu toolchain and AVR libraries. The Atmel development Studio can also be used. Arduino programs are written in a variant of c/c++. There is a large ecosystem of Arduino code available on the web.

The Arduino hardware reference designs are distributed under an Open Source Creative Commons Attribution Share-Alike 2.5 license and are available on the Arduino Web site. Layout and production files for some versions of the Arduino hardware are also available. The source code for the IDE and the on-board library are available and released under the GPLv2 license. The Arduino design has influenced many other similar devices.

The ARM processor has taken an impressive place in the embedded microcontroller world. The Roomba is based on the ARM architecture.

The Stellaris LM3S9B92 Evalbot Robot Evaluation Board is an ARM-based architecture with an embedded controller, motors, sensors, power and communications. The device has usb connectivity to a host development system. Three AA size batteries power the platform. It is priced around $150.

The processor, the TI LM3S9B92 microcontroller chip uses the ARM Cortex-3 core plus the Thumb-2 instruction set. It is a member of TI's STellaris product family. It implements single-cycle hardware multiply and divide, and supports unaligned data access. It has separate buses for instructions and data. Interrupt handling is deterministic, always being 12 cycles. Memory protection is provided. The chip is optimized for single-cycle flash memory. It supports a 80-MHz clock. It has a 24-bit integrated system timer, a vectored interrupt controller with an NMI and dynamically re-prioritizable interrupts.

The microcontroller includes 96 kBytes of single cycle RAM on chip and 256 kBytes of single cycle flash. Flash blocks of 1-kbyte in size can be marked as read-only or execute-only. The I/O can support 10/100 Ethernet, 2 CAN controllers, USB 2.0, three UART's, dual I²C, and dual synchronous serial. There are four 32-bit timers, eight PWM's, two watchdog timers, and up to 65 general purpose I/O's. Two quadrature encoder inputs are provided for motor feedback. There are two 10-bit A/D's with 16 shared channels. In additional, there are three analog comparators that can generate an interrupt. JTAG is supported.

The robot platform enhances this with a connector for a MicroSD card for bulk storage,an audio codec with speaker, using the I2S connection, and RJ-45 ethernet connector, future expansion for wireless, a small OLED display, two dc motors, wheel rotation sensors, bump sensors, and a variety of other sensor units that can be added.

The software environment, hosted in an external pc, is based on one of five industry standard ARM IDE's.

Reference: www.ti.com/evalbot.

The Raspberry Pi

The Raspberry Pi is a small, inexpensive, single board computer based on the ARM architecture. It is targeted to the academic market. It uses the Broadcom BCM2835 system-on-a-chip, which has a 700 MHz ARM processor, a video GPU, and currently 512 M of RAM. It uses an SD card for storage. The Raspberry Pi runs the GNU/linux and FreeBSD operating systems. It was first sold in February 2012. Sales reached ½ million units by the Fall. Due to the open source nature of the software, Raspberry Pi applications and drivers can be downloaded from various sites. It requires a single power supply, and dissipates less than 5 watts. It has USB ports, and an Ethernet controller. It does not have a real-time clock, but one can easily be added. It outputs video in HDMI resolution, and supports audio output. I/O includes 8 general purpose I/O lines, UART, I2C bus, and SPI bus.

Maple board

The Maple board, from LeafLabs is an Arduino-derived ARM architecture using the STM32F103RBT6, a 32-bit ARM Cortex M3 microprocessor. It is implemented on a 2 x 2 inch board, the design of which is open source. It operates at 72 MHz, and has 128 KB of flash and 20 KB of SRAM. There are 43 general digital I/O pins (GPIOs), 15 PWM pins at 16 bit resolution, and 15 analog input (ADC) pins at 12-bit resolution. It includes dual SPI peripherals, dual I^2C peripherals, seven channels of DMA, and three USART (serial port) peripherals. There is one advanced and three general-purpose timers, and a dedicated USB port for programming and communications, which also supplies power. JTAG support is included. There is a nested vectored interrupt controller (NVIC). The Maple board is small and inexpensive, yet very capable, and a good learned tool for embedded systems. The associated IDE is hosted on a variety of platforms, including Windows, Linux, and Apple. It is Open Source, and has extensive libraries. The Maple is a good and inexpensive board to play with, and develop hands-on experience with the technology. I use this board in my undergraduate and graduate Embedded Systems classes.

Beaglebone

The Beaglebone board is open source hardware. It has a 1-gigahertz 32-bit ARM cpu. It can run operating systems such as Linux, bsd, and Android. It can use flash memory cards of (currently) 4 gigabytes. It has a series of standard interfaces like usb, Ethernet, and video, and has expandable I/O. For languages, it supports JavaScript, C, and Python. Support boards are available with a wide variety of sensors.

This board is built around the Texas Instrument's OMAP3530 system-on-a-chip. It includes an ARM Cortex A8 cpu and a TI TMS320C64x+ Digital Signal Processor, and there is a 2D/3D rendering engine for graphics. It supports usb, RS-232, JTAG, and audio in/out, as well as an S-video and HDMI port. There is 256 megabytes of RAM, and 256 Megabytes of flash. It boots from ROM. The original cpu speed was 730 MHz, but the latest models feature a 1 Ghz cpu.

Software

This section discusses software for personal robotic systems. As hardware for robotics systems becomes more "off the shelf," the software gets more attention. Good engineers are not necessarily good programmers. Software, too, has become more off the shelf, with operating systems and extensive libraries of useful routines designed for reuse.

I have always been a proponent of the robot hosting its own development environment. Now, there are enough resources on the mobile robot to support this.

There is a variety of off-the-shelf software solutions for the small embedded processors boards. You don't have to ask, "what language do I program that in?" The choices are c-like and Java-like. Generally, you get an Integrated Development Environment that allows you to stitch together routines from code libraries. Sometimes, you can do this graphically. You are also capable of using the traditional coding model, for high level languages or assembly. There are many third-party development platforms that address coding across platforms.

The Integrated Development Environment (IDE) is a software tool, generally hosted on a pc, to develop, download, ad test code on the target embedded system. The IDE is used to produce code for embedded systems. This is a set of tools for compilation, debugging, simulation, and code version control.

Usually, a rich selection of library routines are provided as well. IDE's usually include a source code editor. Some IDE's support multiple languages. The output of the IDE will be a code "load" that can be sent to the embedded system, or put into a non-volatile memory. An IDE, hosted on a desktop machine with a large set of resources, represents a cross-tool for embedded target code development. Web-based IDE's are emerging. These run in a standard browser.

Keep in mind, executing software consumes energy and requires time. This can be observed and measured. A key issue is the development of a program style, and the development of a programming mindset; specifically. how will I debug this? This is the Design for Testability approach. It is similar to the Design for Test approach in hardware, where test points are provided at the design level.

It is critically important to document at development time. You won't have time later in the design process. The documentation can flow from requirements to specification to implementation and test. In fact, it is possible to write the documentation before the software code. It will need to be updated later to match reality, of course.

Another good practice is to define data structures first, then the processing. We all tend to focus on the algorithm first, but clever choices of data structures will simplify the algorithm. If shortcuts are required for speed or space, be sure to document your assumptions, and your violations.

Libraries of code to address specific functions; device drivers, and other software is generally available. It is always good to check whether the software function you need has already be done. It is worth a day of research, downloading, and testing to save time. However, readily available software doesn't always fit your specific problem. It is generally poorly documented, and it may contain malware.

Purchasing software from an established vendor provides some level of trustworthiness but doesn't guarantee success. Look for software modules and libraries that are supported. Software tools are also available in proprietary and open source versions.

Open Source versus Proprietary

This is a topic we need to discuss before we get very far into software. It is not a technical topic, but concerns your right to use (and/or own, modify) software. It's those software licenses you click to agree with, and never read. That's what the intellectual property lawyers are betting on.

Software and software tools are available in proprietary and open source versions. Open source software is free and widely available, and may be incorporated into your system. It is available under license, which generally says that you can use it, but derivative products must be made available under the same license. This presents a problem if it is mixed with purchased, licensed commercial software, or a level of exclusivity is required. Major government agencies such as the Department of Defense and NASA have policies related to the use of Open Source software.

Adapting a commercial or open source operating system to a particular problem domain can be tricky. Usually, the commercial operating systems need to be used "as-is" and the source code is not available. The software can usually be configured between well-defined limits, but there will be no visibility of the internal workings. For the open source situation, there will be a multitude of source code modules and libraries that can be configured and customized, but the process is complex. The user can also write new modules in this case.

Large corporations or government agencies sometimes have problems incorporating open source products into their projects. Open Source did not fit the model of how they have done business traditionally. They are issues and lingering doubts. Many Federal agencies have developed Open Source policies. NASA has created an open source license, the NASA Open Source Agreement (NOSA), to address these issues. It has released software under this license, but the Free Software Foundation had some issues with the terms of the license. The Open Source Initiative (www.opensource.org) maintains the definition of Open Source, and certifies licenses such as the NOSA.

The GNU General Public License (GPL) is the most widely used free software license. It guarantees end users the freedoms to use, study, share, copy, and modify the software. Software that ensures that these rights are retained is called free software. The license was originally written by Richard Stallman of the Free Software Foundation (FSF) for the GNU project in 1989. The GPL is a *copyleft* license, which means that derived works can only be distributed under the same license terms. This is in distinction to permissive free software licenses, of which the BSD licenses are the standard examples. Copyleft is in counterpoint to traditional copyright. Proprietary software "poisons" free software, and cannot be included or integrated with it, without abandoned the GPL. The GPL covers the GNU/linux operating systems and most of the GNU/linux-based applications.

A Vendor's software tools and operating system or application code is usually proprietary intellectual property. It is unusual to get the source code to examine, at least without binding legal documents and additional funds. Along with this, you do get the vendor support. An alternative is open source code, which is in the public domain. There are a series of licenses covering open source code usage, including the Creative Commons License, the gnu public license, copyleft, and others. Open Source describes a collaborative environment for development and testing. Use of open source code carries with it an implied responsibility to "pay back" to the community. Open Source is not necessarily free.

The Open source philosophy is sometimes at odds with the rigidized procedures evolved to ensure software performance and reliability. Offsetting this is the increased visibility into the internals of the software packages, and control over the entire software package. Besides application code, operating systems such as GNU/linux and bsd can be open source. The programming language Python is open source. The popular web server Apache is also open source.

Languages

The *c language* is an ANSI and ISO standard. Many embedded C environments differ from pure ANSI C, and only provide subsets of the language. They also provide extensions which allow more direct control over hardware. Aspects of C which do not fit target architecture well are left out.

Java is an object-oriented language with a syntax similar to that of c. The language is compiled to bytecodes which are executed by a Java Virtual Machine (JVM). The JVM is hosted on the computer hardware, and is an instruction interpreter program. Thus, the Java language is independent of the hardware it executes on. The JVM has also been instantiated directly in hardware.

The *JVM* is a software environment that allows bytecodes to be executed. There are standard libraries to implement the applications programming interface (API). These implement the Java runtime environment. Other languages besides Java can be compiled into bytecode, notably Pascal, ADA, and Python. JVM is written in the c language.

The JVM can emulate and interpret the instruction set, or use a technique called *Just in Time* (JIT) compilation. The latter approach provides greater speed. The JVM also validates the bytecodes before execution.

The bytecode is interpreted or compiled. Java includes an API to make up the Java runtime environment. Oracle Corporation owns Java, but allows use of the trademark, as long as the products adhere to the JVM Specification. The JVM implements a stack-based architecture. Code executes as privileged or unprivileged, which limits access to some resources.

Python is a general purpose higher order language. It is open source, and designed to be highly readable. It comes with most Gnu-Linux distributions now. There are many interpreters and compilers available for Python. It can be used as an object-oriented or function/procedural language. Python has expressions similar to those of Java, and there is a large standard library of routines.

In embedded, you are working closer to the hardware. At times, you may need to delve into assembly language. You may need to write a device driver (horrors!). As opposed to general languages such as c or Java, the assembly language is unique to the hardware architecture. The concepts are generally the same across assemblers for different architectures. A statement in assembly usually maps directly to one machine language instruction, where a statement in a higher order language would result in multiple machine language instructions.

Operating systems

An *operating system* (OS) is a software program that manages computer hardware and software resources, and provides common services for execution of various application programs. Without an operating system, a user cannot run an application program on their computer, unless the application program is itself self-booting. And that's the key for simple applications. You don't need an operating system, but your code has to include some of its functionality. In some IDE's the operating system code is attached to you code, behind your back. You may not be aware its there. Your scheduler module can be a simple "do" loop. Don't over-complicate things.

For hardware functions such as input, output, and memory allocation, the operating system acts as an intermediary between application programs and the computer hardware, although the application code is usually executed directly by the hardware and will frequently call the OS or be interrupted by it. Operating systems are found on almost any device that contains a computer. The operating system functions need to be addressed by software (or possibly hardware), even if there is no entity that we can point to, called the Operating System. In simple, usually single-task programs, there might not be an operating system per se, but the functionality is still part of the overall software.

An operating system manages computer resources, including:

- Memory.
- I/O.
- Interrupts.
- Tasks/processes/application programs.

The operating system arbitrates and enforces priorities. If there are not multiple software entities to arbitrate among, the job is simpler. An operating system can be off-the-shelf commercial or open source code, or the application software developer can decide to build his or her own. To avoid unnecessary reinvention of the wheel an available product is usually chosen. Operating systems are usually large and complex pieces of software. This is because they have to be generic in function, as the originator does not know what application space it will be used in. Operating systems for desktop/network/server application are usually not applicable for embedded applications. Mostly they are too large, having many components that will not be needed (such as the human interface), and they do not address the real-time requirements of the embedded domain.

Adapting a commercial or open source operating system to a particular embedded domain can be tricky. Usually, the commercial operating systems need to be used "as-is" and the source code is not available. The software can usually be configured between well-defined limits, but there will be no visibility of the internal workings. For the open source situation, there will be a multitude of source code modules and libraries that can be configured and customized, but the process is complex. The user can also write new modules in this case.

Operating Systems designed for the desktop are not necessarily suited to the embedded space. There were developed under the assumption that whatever memory is required will be available, and real-time operation with hard deadlines is not required.

Real-time operating systems, as opposed to those addressing desktop, tablet, and server applications, emphasize predictability and consistency rather than throughput and low latencies.

Determinism is probably the most important feature in a real-time operating system.

A microkernel operating system is ideally suited to embedded systems. It is slimmed down to include only those features needed, with no additional code. Barebones is the term sometimes used. The microkernel handles memory management, threads, and communication between processes. It has device drivers for only those devices present. The operating systems may have to be recompiled when new devices are added. A file system, if required, is run in user space. MINIX, as an example of a streamlined kernel, has about 6,000 lines of code.

Some example off-the-shelf operating systems include:

Android

The *Android* operating system by Google has found application in numerous smartphone and tablet computers since its introduction in 2008. It is an Open Source product based on Gnu-Linux, although not all of the code is covered by Open Source licenses. It has evolved into versions for set-top boxes, robotics, digital cameras, and digital television applications. Android supports several hardware computing platforms including ARM, POWER, x86, and MIPS.

Like Java, Android provides a virtual machine execution engine for a specific hardware platform. This virtual machine is termed Dalvik. It's strengths are in memory-limited systems, and those with hard real time requirements. Android is targeted to user input from touch, with a screen using icons. In an embedded application, it may have no direct user interface. Android uses the Gnu-Linux kernel, plus middleware, libraries of code, and API's. The user community supports a large library of applications for Android. Android has built-in support for power management.

Real Time and embedded Linux

There are several approaches to make GNU/Linux a real-time operating system. One version developed by FSM labs, and used by VxWorks, is a hard real-time RTOS microkernel that runs the entire Gnu-Linux operating system as a fully preemptive process. To address soft real-time, the GNU/Linux kernel can be modified by several available patches to add non-preemption and low latency, with a deterministic scheduler.

The standard GNU/Linux (or BSD) kernel is not pre-emptable. This means kernel code runs to completion. The run time is not bounded, which interferes with responding to time-critical events. It is important to keep in mind that the Gnu-Linux kernel was not designed for non-preemption, as a true real-time operating system would be. Preemption has overhead, and influences throughput, usually adversely. There is a real-time Linux Foundation (.org) that is a good source of information on these topics.

Ubuntu Mobile and Embedded are variations of the Ubuntu Linux distribution for Mobile Phones, and embedded applications in general.

LynxOS

The LynxOS RTOS is a Unix-like real-time operating system from LynuxWorks It is a real-time POSIX operating system for embedded applications. LynxOS components are designed for absolute determinism (hard real-time performance), which means that they respond within a known period of time. Predictable response times are ensured even in the presence of heavy I/O due to the kernel's unique threading model, which allows interrupt routines to be extremely short and fast. LynuxWorks has a specialized version of LynxOS called LynxOS-178, especially for use in avionics applications that require certification to industry standards such as DO-178B.

QNX

QNX is a real-time operating system based on Unix. QNX Neutrino RTOS is SMP capable, and supports POSIX APIs. It is not open source.

The QNX microkernel contains only CPU scheduling, inter-process communication, interrupt redirection, and timers. Everything else runs as a user process, including a special process known as *proc,* which performs process creation, and memory management by operating in conjunction with the microkernel. There are no device drivers in the kernel. The network stack is based on NetBSD code.

RTEMS

RTEMS is the Real-Time Executive for Multiprocessor Systems, designed for embedded use, and free and open source. It is POSIX compliant. The TCP/IP stack from FreeBSD is included. RTEMS does not provide memory management, but is single process, multithreaded. Numerous file systems are supported. RTEMS is available for the ARM, Atmel AVR, and a wide variety of other popular embedded cpu's and DSP's. An RTEMS system is currently in orbit around Mars.

RTOS

In a real-time system, the timing of the result is as important as the logical correctness. Embedded systems find themselves in these situations a lot. There are two types of deadlines, hard and soft, and various scheduling policies to address these. A scheduling policy should have the ability to meet all deadlines. The scheduling overhead should be minimal.

In soft real time, the average performance or response time is emphasized. Desktops and servers can meet soft real time requirements. Missing a deadline is not necessarily catastrophic. Embedded examples include an elevator controller, vending machines, gas pumps, cash registers and POS, thermostats, mobile phones, and a bike computer. Missing a deadline may result in a degradation of service, but not a failure.

In hard real time, on the other hand, critical sections of code have absolute deadlines, regardless of how busy the system is. Missing a deadline means system failure. Response times must be deterministic. Examples of hard real time systems include avionics fly-by-wire system, antilock brakes, stability control in automotive applications, and nuclear power plant safety systems.

Interestingly, meeting a deadline early may be just as bad as meeting it late. There are constraint requirements on the response time for the systems.

We can have systems with the characteristics of both; these multi-rate systems handle operations and deadlines at varying rates.

Non-Real Time (NRT) systems are fair; they provide resources (time, I/O) to all users or programs on an equal, or pre-determined priority basis. They can arbitrate resource allocation to maximize the number of deadlines met, or minimize lateness, or some combination. Everyone gets a turn. NRT systems have high throughput and fast average response.

File Systems

A file system provides a way to organize data in a standard format. An embedded system, like a digital camera, can store and organize its data (photos) and exchange the data directly with a computer. The file system stores the data, and metadata (data about the data) such as date, time, permissions, etc. Some operating systems support multiple file systems.

The important thing about a file systems for embedded systems is, don't reinvent the wheel! There are many good file systems out there, and the provide a compatibility across platforms.

The DOS file system

The legacy disk operating system (DOS) file structure is built upon linked lists. The directory file contains lists of files and information about them. It uses a 32-byte entry per file, containing the file name, extension, attributes, date and time, and the starting location of the file on disk.

The File Allocation Table (FAT) is a built map of allocated clusters on the disk. A cluster is the default unit of storage. It's size is a trade-off between efficiency of storage, and efficiency of access. A size of 256 bytes to 1024 bytes worked well in the early days. Two copies of the FAT are kept by the system, and these are on fixed locations of the storage media.

A directory file has entries for all of the files on the disk. The name of the file is in 8.3 format, meaning an 8 character file name, and a

3-character extension. The extension tells the type of the file, executable program, word processing, etc. By DOS convention, when a file is erased, the first character of the name is changed to the character E516. The data is not lost at this point. If nothing else happens in the mean-time, the file can be un-erased, and recovered. However, the E5 signifies the space the file occupied is now available for use.

Various file attribute bits are kept. The file can be marked as read-only, hidden, reserved system type, and bits indicate a directory field, a volume label (name of a storage volume, like, "disk1"), and whether the file has been archived (saved). There is a 16-bit date code in the format (year-1980)*512 + month * 32 + day. (thought exercise – when do we have a problem?). The starting cluster number in a directory is kept as a word value. This limits us to 216 clusters.

The FAT was originally 12-bits, but later extended to 16. Eventually, this was extended to 32-bits for Windows, and is no longer DOS compatible. Entries in the FAT map the clusters on the storage media. These indicate used, available, bad, and reserved clusters.

Linux supports the various versions of the .ext file family.

Apps

The applications, the device software is limited only by imagination. The software development tools are there, and the languages are available. What language should you use to produce software for the robot? Doesn't really matter. What computer languages do you know? C, Java, Python, Logo – whatever you want. Actually, don't use Cobol.

An Architectural Model

NASREM

The NASA/NBS Standard Reference Model for Telerobot Control System Architecture was evolved as a model for the implementation of advanced control architectures.

The NBS architecture is a generic framework in which to implement intelligence of a telerobotic device. It was developed over a decade as part of a research program in industrial robotics at NBS (now. NIST) in which over $25 million was spent. The NBS program involved over fifty professionals and extensive facilities, including robots, a supercomputer, mainframes. minicomputers. microcomputers. LISP machines. and AI workstations. This model, designed originally for industrial robots. is the mechanism by which sensors. expert systems. and controls are linked and operated such that a system behaves with some measure of autonomy, if not intelligence.

Systems designed from this model perform complex real-time tasks in the presence of sensory input from a variety of sensors. They decomposes high level goals into low level actions. making real-time decisions in the presence of noise and conflicting demands on resources. The model provides a framework for linking artificial intelligence. expert system. and neural techniques with classical real-time control. Sensors are interfaced to controls through a hierarchically-structured real-time world model. The world model integrates current sensory data with a priori knowledge to provide the control system with a current best estimate of the state of the system.

NASREM is a generic hierarchical structured functional model for the overall system. The hierarchical nature makes it ideal for

78

telerobot systems, and for gradual evolution of the system. The model also provides a set of common reference terminology, which can enable the construction of a database. It defines interfaces, which allows for modularization. The model allows for evolutionary growth, while providing a structure of the interleaving of human:robotic control.

NASREM's 6-level model operates from a global memory (or database). At each level we have three processes, sensory processing world modeling, and task decomposition (execute). At the very lowest level, we have the raw sensors and the servo systems. Going up from that, we have the primitive level, the elementary move level, the task level, the service bay level, and the mission level. At the servo level, we would find cameras, and their associated pan/tilt control as well as mobility and joint motor control, with associated position feedback. At the primitive move level, we would find the camera subsystem, the arm, the mobility subsystem, and the grippers. At the elementary (or e-) move level, we would find systems such as perception or manipulation. At the task level, we might locate the entire telerobotic system.

The world modeling process starts with a sparse database. Sensor data, appropriate to the level flows in, and there might be a capability for data fusion. A task planner task can make "what-if" queries of the world model (which is state-based). The modeling task uses a global database of state variable, lists, maps and knowledge bases to allow a modeling process to update and predict states, to evaluate current states and possible states, and to report results to a task executor task. The World model, evaluates states, both existing states as evidenced by sensor data, and possible states, as postulated by the task planner.

The timing and time horizon of the various levels of the model is are vastly different. The servo level operates on the millisecond level, the primitive level, at 10's to 100's of milliseconds, and the e-move level at about a one second update interval. It would have about a 30 second planning horizon. The task level would have update interval on the order of seconds to 10's of seconds, with a planning horizon in the 10's of seconds. Moving up, the service by level would update in the 1's of seconds, with a planning horizon the order of minutes to 10's of minutes. Finally, the mission level might update on the order of minutes, with a horizon of an hour.

The servo level would accept Cartesian trajectory points from the next level up, and transform these to drive voltages or current for the mechanisms. The Primitive level would accept pose (or collection of joint angles and positions) information from the next higher level, and generate the Cartesian trajectory point to pass down the hierarchy. These involve dynamics calculations. The e-move level would accept elementary move commands and generate pose commands, after orientations in the coordinate frame, singularities, and clearances. It uses simple if-then state transition rules. The task level, the one the telerobot would be located at, accepts task commands (from the human operator), does subsystem assignments and scheduling, and generates a series of e-moves.

Real Time Control System (RCS)

RCS evolved form NASREM over decades, starting in the 1970's It is currently at RCS Level 4. RCS is a Reference Model Architecture for real-time control. It provides a framework for implementation in terms of a hierarchical control model derived from best theory and best practices. RCS was heavily influenced by the understanding of the biological cerebellum. NIST maintains a library of RCS software listings, scripts and tools, in ADA, Java, and C++.

An abstraction, the perfect joint accepts analog or digital torque commands, and produces the required torque via a dc motor. It also provides state feedback in the form of force, torque, angle or position, (depending on whether the joint configuration is Cartesian or revolute), and possibly rate. The perfect joint includes a pulse width modulator (pwm), a motor, and possibly a gearbox. Internal feedback and compensation is provided to compensate for gearbox or other irregularities such as hysteresis or stiction, For example, the torque pulses common to harmonic drives can be compensated for within the perfect joint. The perfect joint is part of the lowest NASREM level. The processing provided theoretically achieves a "perfect" torque, where the outputted torque matches the commanded torque.

The Individual Joint Controller (IJC) implements a simple control law to allow joint by joint operation of the manipulator.

The IJC provides a functional redundancy to the higher level telerobot control discussed below. The IJC accepts inputs from a kinematic ally similar mini-master controller. This simplifies the computational requirements on the IJC, by removing the need for coordinate transformations. The IJC does not include any dynamic joint coupling compensation. It basically implements seven parallel, non-interacting control laws, that may be simple PD loops. For this case, roughly 140 operations per cycle are required.

The telerobot controller initially implemented the first three NASREM levels, and could accept commands from a joystick-type element, a mini-master, or higher levels of the model. This level required a computational capability of several MIPS, and an accuracy of 32 bits. Floating point capability was assumed. This controller could perform coordinate transformations in real time, although the computation burden argued for a custom hardware approach to this particular subset of the computations.

The telerobot control system implemented the first 3 (of 7) levels of the NASREM model. Further levels could be added later in a phased evolution of the system. For early systems, the human operator provided the functionality of the upper control levels.

Standards

There are many Standards applicable to personal robotic systems. These range from general computer standards to hardware and operational standards. Why should we be interested in standards? Standards represent an established approach, based on best practices. Standards are not created to stifle creativity or direct an implementation approach, but rather to give the benefit of previous experience. Adherence to standards implies that different parts will work together. Standards are often developed by a single company, and then adopted by the relevant industry. Other Standards are imposed by large customer organizations such as the Department of Defense, or the automobile industry. Many standards organizations exist to develop, review, and maintain standards.

Standards exist in many areas, including hardware, software, interfaces, protocols, testing, system safety, security, and certification. Standards can be open or closed (proprietary).

Hardware standards include the form factor and packaging of chips, the electrical interface, the bus interface, the power interface, and others. The JTAG standard specifies an interface for debugging.

In computer architecture, the ISA specifies the instruction set and the operations. It does not specify the implementation. Popular ISA's are x86 (Intel) and ARM (ARM Holdings, LTD). These are proprietary, and licensed by the Intellectual Property holder.

In software, an API (applications program interface) specifies the interface between a user program, and the operating system. To run properly, the program must adhere to the API. POSIX is an IEEE standard for portable operating systems.

Language standards also exist, such as those for the ANSI c and the Java language.

Networking standards include TCP/IP for Ethernet, the CAN bus from Bosch, and IEEE-1553 for avionics.

It is always good to review what standards are and could be applied to an embedded system, as it ensures the application of best practices from experience, and interoperability with other systems.

The Portable Operating System Interface for Unix (POSIX) is an IEEE standard, IEEE 1003.1-1988. The standard spans some 17 documents. POSIX provides a Unix-like environment and API. Various operating systems are certified to POSIX compliance, including BSD, LynxOS, QNX, VxWorks, and others.

Security

Have you been robo-jacked today? All robotic systems have aspects of security. A user's personal data on cell phones is vulnerable. The data on your computer is at risk. Your robot systems cost time and money to build and deploy – it needs protection as well. We are not so much worried that your creation will turn against you, as that it will be used against you and your data.

Robot systems operate in an unfriendly world. They are available to attacks from hacking, viruses and malware, theft, damage, spoofing, and other nasty techniques from the desktop/server world. GPS systems can be hacked to provide incorrect location or critical time information Cell phones and tablets are connected wirelessly to large networks. A bored teenage hacker in Europe took over the city Tram system as his private full-scale railroad, using a TV remote. What about the teenager in an internet café is a third-world country. They would derive much amusement from making your robot run amuck.

Some of these issues are addressed by existing protocols and standards for access and communications security. Security may also imply system stability and availability. Standard security measures such as security reviews and audits, threat analyses, target and threat assessments, countermeasures deployment, and extensive testing apply to the embedded domain.

The completed functional system may need additional security features, such as intrusion detection, data encryption, and perhaps a self-destruct capability. Is that self-destruct capability secure, so not just anyone can activate it? All of these additional features use time, space, and other resources that are usually scarce in small embedded systems for robotics.

Techniques such as hard checksums and serial numbers are one approach to device protection. Access to the system needs to be controlled. If unused ports exist, the corresponding device drivers should be disabled, or not included. Mechanisms built into the cpu hardware can provide protection of system resources such as memory.

Security has to be designed in from the very beginning; it can't just be added on. Memorize this. Even the most innocuous embedded platform in a small robot can be used as a springboard to penetrate other systems.

<u>Safety</u>

Mobile Robotic systems operate in the real world, and the real world can be scary. We need to be aware of the hazards that a mobile robot systems can present to others, and the hazards it itself can be subject to. We have covered some of those in the section on security. A good starting point for robotic safety comes from a science fiction book published in 1942 by Isaac Asimov. In his short story, *Runaround*, he introduced his *Three Laws of Robotics,* which have stood the test of time. From their introduction in speculative fiction to their influence on industrial systems, they are well-thought-out.

And, they are:

- A robot may not injure a human being or, through inaction, allow a human being to come to harm.

- A robot must obey the orders given to it by human beings, except where such orders would conflict with the First Law.

- A robot must protect its own existence as long as such protection does not conflict with the First or Second Law.

Asimov went on to write many robotics stories, where the effect of the three laws were seen in some unusual situations. He actually attributes the formulation of his laws to a discussion with John

Campbell in 1940. Asimov always assumed the robots he wrote about had inherent safeguards.

So, based on Asimov's laws as a starting point, we can derive some requirements for our personal robotic systems. First, to not harm a human, the robot must have passive and active safety systems. It must be aware of humans within its reach or task space. Speaking as one who was pinned to a wall by a 350 pound robot cart, a human-sensor is a good idea. If you are operating your quadcopter, it is not a good idea to fly it into another person (dog, car...). The flow-down safety from the 3-laws continue. Consider safe design, and safe operation at the beginning.

Where's the dream?

Has there been any progress in the last thirty years in the field of personal robots? Yes, but...the R2D2 functionality still alludes us. The computer power is available. Walking, swimming, flying and manipulating subsystems are off-the-shelf. Communications technologies such as WiFi and bluetooth are readily available. Memory is, for practical purposes, free. Secondary storage using low-power solid state disks is readily available and cheap. Access to the Web and the Cloud is enabled by wireless networking. This means a lot of the intelligence does not need to be hosted onboard the robot. Batteries are much better with higher energy density with such units as Lithium-ion.

Development systems and languages remain a hurdle, but are getting better. The parts and subsystems are available, and the interest level is, if anything, higher that it ever was before.

Where are the drivers and the enablers today for personal robotics?

Today (circa 2014) with better, cheaper, and more capable building blocks, colleges and high schools are working on their own satellites (Cubesats) as well as high altitude balloon missions. They are deeply into robotics. Some of the programs are discussed below.

Google Lunar X-Prize

This is a lunar robotics competition, organized by the X-Prize Foundation in 2007, and is valid through 2015. It requires a team to develop and demonstrate a robot on the moon that travels at least 500 meters, and transmits back high definition video. The prize for this is $20 million. If accomplished, this would be the first vehicle to operate on the lunar surface since 1976, and the first non-governmental effort. Another goal is to capture images of Apollo hardware on the moon, verifying the presence of water ice, or surviving through the 2-week long lunar night.

This effort was originally to be funded by NASA, but that would have limited the competition to United States Teams. The X-Prize Foundation, funded by Google, has no such restrictions. More than thirty international teams are officially working on this effort.

Reference:
Alicia Chang (2007-09-14). "Google to Finance Moon Challenge Contest". . Washington Post

STEM

STEM stands for science, technology, engineering, and mathematics. The STEM fields are those academic and professional disciplines that fall under the umbrella areas represented by the acronym. According to both the United States National Research Council (NRC) and the National Science Foundation (NSF), the fields are collectively considered core technological underpinnings of an advanced society. In many forums (including political/governmental and academic) the strength of the STEM workforce is viewed as an indicator of a nation's ability to sustain itself.

The Science, Technology, Engineering, and Mathematics Education Coalition works to support STEM programs for teachers and students at the U. S. Department of Education, the National Science Foundation, and other agencies that offer STEM related programs.

FIRST

FIRST (For Inspiration and Recognition of Science and Technology) is an organization founded by inventor Dean Kamen in 1989 to develop ways to inspire students in engineering and technology fields. The organization is the foundation for the FIRST Robotics Competition, FIRST LEGO League, Junior FIRST LEGO League, and FIRST Tech Challenge competitions.

The FIRST® LEGO® League is an international competition organized by FIRST for elementary and middle school students. Each year, a new challenge is announced that focuses on a different real-world topic related to the sciences. The robotics part of the competition revolves around designing and programming LEGO Robots to complete tasks. The students work out solutions to the various problems they are given and then meet for regional tournaments to share their knowledge, compare ideas, and display their robots. FIRST LEGO League is a partnership between FIRST and the LEGO Group. It also has a scaled-down robotics program for children ages 6–9 called Junior FIRST LEGO League.

Zero Robotics Competition

This program involves a series of robots already on the International Space Station called SPHERES (Synchronized

Position Hold, Engage, Reorient Experimental Satellites). These have a mass of around ten pounds, and a diameter of 8 inches. They use twelve CO_2 thrusters for movement, and are battery powered. They were developed at the MIT Space systems Laboratory as a testbed for control, autonomy, and metrology for distributed spacecraft and docking missions. The SPHERES were inspired by the Training Remotes from the Star Wars films. There are three SPHERES, in different colors.

As a team, they can control their relative their relative position and orientation. They had been tested aboard KC-135 aircraft flying zero-gravity flight paths, and were delivered to the International Space Station (ISS) in 2006.

The NASA/MIT Competition allows teams to develop software for the SPHERES, and test it in a simulation environment. Selected teams test their software on SPHERES in an air-bearing floor facility. In December 2011, a few teams will test their code and algorithms in the SPHERES onboard the ISS.

On your own

Here are some suggested approaches to inexpensive personal robot projects you can do on your own. Also, check local high schools and colleges for robotics clubs and programs. If you are experienced, volunteer as a mentor. If you are starting out new, it is good to work with a group of like-minded individuals. First, understand your strengths and weaknesses. Are you a computer hardware person, a software person, a mechanical person, or none of the above. Play to your strengths, but tackle your technical weaknesses. Take classes, Explore programming environments. See what projects people are working on, using the web as a resource. To start, you might want to get an electric radio controlled truck, car, plane, quadcopter, boat, or submarine. That gives you a platform to start with. Now, what can adding a small embedded computer buy you?

You could work it the other way. Start with a task that you want to robot to do, and define a platform to do that task. Robot lawn mower? That's commercially available. Service robots for the elderly and disabled? That's an active research area. A telepresense robot that can allow you to be in two places at once? There are some of those, based on tablet computers for control. There are no limits here but your imagination. Best of luck.

Glossary of Terms

Actuator – device which converts a control signal to a mechanical action.

A/D, ADC – analog to digital converter.

ALU – arithmetic logic unit.

Analog – concerned with continuous values.

And – logical operation that is true when both inputs are true.

Android, an Operating system, also a term for a humanoid robot.

Ap – application software, computer program.

Apache – an open source web server.

API – applications programming interface.

Arduino – open source, single board microcontroller using an Atmel AVR (8-bit risc)
        cpu.

ARM – Acorn RISC machine; a 32-bit architecture with wide application in embedded
        systems.

ASIMO – Japanese robot, Advanced Step in Innovative Mobility.

Async – asynchronous; 2 processes not sharing the same clock.

AVR – a microprocessor architecture from Atmel.

BASIC – a simple computer language.

Battlebot – Television show featuring remote controlled armed and armored robots.

Baud – symbol rate; may or may not be the same as bit rate.

Binary – using base 2 arithmetic for number representation.

Bit – 2 state element. Smallest element of the binary system.

Bluetooth – short range radio communications for data.

BoB – personal robot, "brains on board."

BSD – Berkeley Software Distribution version of the Bell Labs Unix operating system.

BSP – board support package; information and drivers for a specific circuit board.

Bus – data channel, communication pathway for data transfer.

Byte – ordered collection of 8 bits; values from 0-255.

bytecodes – computer instruction set designed to be executed by an interpreter program.

c – computer language.

CAN – controller area network.

CD – compact disk (optical media).

Chip – integrated circuit component.

Clock – periodic timing signal to control and synchronize operations.

CMOS – complementary metal oxide semiconductor; a technology using both positive and negative semiconductors to achieve low power operation.

Codec – coder/decoder.

Control Flow – computer architecture involving directed flow through the program; data dependent paths are allowed.

Copyleft – open source license.

Cots – commercial, off-the-shelf.

Courseware – material for a class.

CPU – central processing unit.

Cubesat – a small research satellite (volume = 1 liter), widely used by colleges and individuals.

Dalvik – the Android virtual machine.

DC – direct current.

Device driver – specific software to interface a peripheral to the operating system.

Dram – dynamic random access memory.

Droid – robot.

Drone – unmanned aerial vehicle.

DSP – digital signal processing.

DVD – optical media, "digital video disk"

Embedded system – a computer systems with limited human interfaces and performing specific tasks. Usually part of a larger system.

Endian – which side of the digital word has the least significant bit.

Eprom – erasable programmable read-only memory.

Ethernet – networking protocol for wired or wireless data networks.

Firmware – code contained in a non-volatile memory.

Flag – a binary indicator.

Flash memory – a type of non-volatile memory, similar to Eeprom.

Flip-flop – device that can be in one of two states.

Floating point – computer numeric format for real numbers; has significant digits and an exponent.

FPGA – field programmable gate array.

FPU – floating point unit, an ALU for floating point numbers.

Full duplex – communication in both directions simultaneously.

Gate – a circuit to implement a logic function; can have multiple inputs, but a single output.

Giga - 10^9 or $2^{30.}$

GHz – giga ($10^{9)}$ hertz.

GPIO – general purpose input output.

GPS – global positioning system (U.S.) system of navigation satellites.

GPU – graphics processing unit. ALU for graphics data.

GUI – graphics user interface.

Hero – a series of robots from heath corporation in the 1980's.

Hotplug – to connect equipment without turning the power off first.

Hz – Hertz, or cycles per second.

IDE – integrated device electronics – an interface for storage devices.

IEEE – Institute of Electrical and Electronic Engineers. Professional organization and standards body.

Integer – the natural numbers, zero, and the negatives of the natural numbers.

Interrupt – an asynchronous event to signal a need for attention (example: the phone rings).

I/O – Input-output from the computer to external devices, or a user interface.

IoT – Internet of Things.

IP – intellectual property; also internet protocol.

IoT – Internet of Things.

IR – infrared, 1-400 terahertz. Perceived as heat.

IPRC – International Personal Robotics Conference.

iRobot – manufacturer of military and civilian robots.

isa – instruction set architecture.

Java – computer language.

Javascript – a scripting language; usually runs in a browser.

Joystick – human interface device for rotation and direction control. Used in aircraft and video games.

JTAG – Joint Test Action Group; industry group that lead to IEEE 1149.1, Standard Test Access Port and Boundary-Scan Architecture.

JVM – Java Virtual Machine – software that allows any architecture to execute Java bytecodes by emulation.

Kbyte – kilo (thousand) bytes.

Kernel – main portion of the operating system. Interface between the applications and the hardware.

Kilo – a prefix for 10^3 or 2^{10}

lamp – linux, apache, MySQL, Python software suite.

lan – local area network.

Lego – Danish maker of building block toys, now involved in robotics as well.

Linux – open source operating system.

LioP – lithium polymer battery.

Logo – programming language for education and robotics, based on LISP (1967).

LUT – look up table.

Malware – malicious software.

Math operation – generally, add, subtract, multiply, divide.

Mbyte – mega (million) bytes.

MEMS – Micro Electronic Mechanical System.

Metadata – data about data; for example, the date and time embedded in a file.

Metaprogramming – programs that produce or modify other programs.

Metrology – science of measurement.

MHz – mega (million) Hertz.

Middleware – software between the operating system, and the applications.

Microcode – hardware level data structures to translate machine instructions into sequences of circuit level operations.

Mindstorm – robotic building blocks from Lego.

Mips – millions of instructions per second.

Microcontroller – microprocessor with included memory and/or I/O.

Microkernel – operating system which is not monolithic. So functions execute in user space.

Microprocessor – a monolithic cpu on a chip.

Milliamp – 10^{-3} amp.

MIPS – millions of instructions per second; sometimes used as a measure of throughput.

MMU – memory management unit; translates virtual to physical addresses.

Multicore – multiple processing cores on one substrate or chip; need not be identical.

MySQL – open source relational database.

NASA – National Aeronautics and Space Administration.

NASREM - NASA/NBS Standard Reference Model for Telerobot Control System Architecture.

NBS – National Bureau of Standards, now NIST.

NIC – network interface connection.

NIST – National Institutes of Standards and Technology.

NMI – non-maskable interrupt; cannot be ignored by the software.

NOP – no operation.

NBS - National Bureau of Standards, now NIST.

NVM – non-volatile memory.

OBD – On-Board diagnostics; for automobiles, a state-of-health systems for emissions control.

Opcode – part of a machine language instruction that specifies the operation to be performed.

Open source – methodology for hardware or software development with free distribution and access.

Operating system – software that controls the allocation of resources in a computer.

Or – logical operation whose output is true when either or both inputs are true.

Paradigm shift – a change from one paradigm to another. Disruptive or evolutionary.

Parallel – multiple operations or communication proceeding s simultaneously.

Parity – an error detecting mechanism involving an extra check bit in the word.

PC – personal computer; push cart.

PDA – personal digital assistant; pocket-sized device; palmtop; 1984; superseded by functions in mobile phones.

PHP – open source scripting language.

PLC – Programmable logic controller, embedded device for automation.

PLD– programmable logic device; generic gate-level part that can be programmed for a function.

PROM – programmable read-only memory.

PWM – pulse width modulation. DC motor speed control technique.

Python – programming language.

Quadrature encoder – an incremental rotary encoder providing rotational position information.

Quadcopter – a small aircraft with four small horizontal rotors, like a helicopter.

Raspberry Pi – a small and inexpensive computer board that hosts the Linux operating system.

RAM – random access memory; any item can be accessed in the same time as any other.

RCS – robot control system.

Reset – signal and process that returns the hardware to a known, defined state.

ROM – read only memory.

ROOMBA – a small floor cleaning robot.

RTOS – real-time operating system.

Sandbox – an isolated and controlled environment to run untested or potentially malicious code.

SATA – serial interface for mass storage devices.

SCADA – Supervisory Control and Data Acquisition – for industrial control systems.

SD – secure digital, non-volatile memory card.

Sensor – a device that converts a physical observable quantity or e vent to a signal.

Serial – bit by bit.

Servo – a control device with feedback.

Siri – voice recognition ap.

Smartphone – communication device, usually running an operating system, with numerous features such as location finding, a camera, etc.

SOC – system on chip.

Software – series of instructions for a computer; description of an algorithm or process.

SRAM – static random access memory.

Stack – first in, last out data structure. Can be hardware or software.

Stack pointer – a reference pointer to the top of the stack.

State machine – model of sequential processes.

Stiction – static friction; needs to be overcome to get started.

System – a collection of interacting elements and relationships with a specific behavior.

System of Systems – a complex collection of systems with pooled resources.

Telerobot – robot system operated remotely.

Thread – smallest independent set of instructions managed by a multiprocessing operating system.

Toolchain – set of programming tools.

TOPO – a personal robot.

Transceiver – receiver and transmitter in one box.

TTL – transistor-transistor logic in digital integrated circuits.

Tri-state – in microelectronic logic families, the output can be "1", "0", or a high impedance.

UART – universal asynchronous receiver-transmitter. Parallel-to-serial; serial-to parallel device with handshaking.

USB – universal serial bus.

Watchcat – watches the watchdog.

Watchdog – hardware/software function to sanity check the hardware, software, and process; applies corrective action if a fault is detected; fail-safe mechanism.

Webcam – small digital camera with network capability.

WiFi – short range radio-based networking.
Wlan – wireless local area network.
Xor – exclusive logical or – true when either but not both inputs
  are true.

Bibliography

Personal Robots

Abut, Huseyin (ed.) et all *Advances for In-Vehicle and Mobile Systems: Challenges for International Standards* Springer; 1 edition, 2007, ISBN-1 038733503X.

Ahn, Ho Seo; Sa, In-Kyu; Choi, Jin Young; *PDA-Based Mobile Robot System with Remote Monitoring for Home Environment*, 2009, Sungkyunkwan University, avail. IEEE Xplore.

Albus, James S., *Brains, Behavior, & Robotics*, McGraw-Hill, 1981, ISBN 0-07-000975-9.

Albus, James S.; *Engineering of Mind: An Introduction to the Science of Intelligent Systems*, Wiley-Interscience; (September 7, 2001), ISBN 0471438545.

Albus, James S. and Meystel, Alesander M.; *Intelligent Systems: Architecture Design*, Control, Wiley-Interscience; August 2001, ISBN 0471193747.

Andersson, Russell L., *A Robot Ping-Pong Player*, MIT Press, 1988, ISBN 0-262-01101-8.

Annan, David, "*Robot, the Mechanical Monster*", Bounty Books, 1976, ISBN 0-517-525992.

Asimov, Isaac and Frenkel, Karen A. *Robots Machines in Man's Image,* 1985, Crown Publishers, Inc. ISBN 0-517-55110-1.

Benedettelli, Daniele *The LEGO MINDSTORMS EV3 Laboratory: Build, Program, and Experiment with Five Wicked Cool Robots!* No Starch Press; 1st ed, 2013, ISBN- 1593275331

100

Boyet, Howard *Hero 1 - Advanced Programming Experiments*, Heathkit/Zenith 1984. ISBN 0871190362.

Bradbeer, Robin *Personal Robot Book*, 1985, Duckworth Publications, ISBN 0715618512.

Bräunl, Thomas; *Embedded Robotics: Mobile Robot Design and Applications with Embedded Systems* Springer; 2nd ed. edition (July 28, 2006) ISBN-3540343180.

RB5X, Byte Magazine, Jan 1984, p. 123-131.

Capek, Karel R.U. R. *Rossum's Universal Robots*, Stage Play, reprinted 2010, Echo Library, 140686711X.

Castellanos, Jose A.; Tardós,, Juan D. *Mobile Robot Localization and Map Building: A Multisensor Fusion Approach,* Springer; 2000 ed , 2000, ISBN- 0792377893 .

Cook, Gerald *Mobile Robots: Navigation, Control and Remote Sensing,* Wiley-IEEE Press; 1st ed, 2011, ISBN-0470630213 .

Critchlow, Arthur J., *Introduction to Robotics*, Macmillan Publishing Co., 1985, ISBN 0-02-325590-0.

DaCosta, Frank, *How to Build Your Own Working Robot Pet*, Tab, ISBN 0-8306-1141-X .

Danko, Dan; Mason, Tom *The Official Guide to Battlebots*, Scholastic Paperbacks, 2002, ISBN 0439390001 .

Dilshad, Azhar *Indoor Mobile Robot Localization* Amazon Digital Services, Inc. ASIN B007P5NAGE.

Dudek, Gregory; Jenkin, Michael *Computational Principles of Mobile Robotics* Cambridge University Press; 2nd ed, 2010, ISBN-0521692121.

Engel, C. William, *The World According to Robo the Robot*, Hayden, 1985, ISBN 0-8104-6331-8.

Escue, Judy, *A Perspective of Personal Robotics*, 1984, Union University, ASIN: B00072ILPC.

Everett, H. R. *Sensors for Mobile Robots*, 1995, CRC Press, ISBN 1568810482.

Everett, Hobart R. "A Microprocessor Controlled Autonomous Sentry Robot," October 1982, Thesis, Navel Postgraduate School, Monterey, CA, A125239.

Graham, Brad; McGowan, Kathy *Build Your Own All-Terrain Robot* McGraw-Hill/TAB Electronics; 1st ed, 2004, ISBN-007143741X.

Ferrari, Mario and Ferrari, Guilio *Building and Programming LEGO Mindstorms Robots Kit,* Syngress, 2002, ISBN-193183671X .

Freedman, Jeri *Robots Through History*, 2011, Rosen Central, ISBN 1448822505.

Ge, Shuzhi Sam *Autonomous Mobile Robots: Sensing, Control, Decision Making and Applications,* CRC Press, 2006, ISBN-0849337488.

Heath, Larry, *Fundamentals of Robotics*, Reston Publishing Co., 1985, ISBN 0-8359-2189-1.

Heath/Zenith Hero Jr. RT-1 Programmers Guide, 1984.

Heath/Zenith Hero Jr. RT-1 Technical Manual, 1984.

Heiserman, David L., *Build Your Own Working Robot*, Tab, 1976, ISBN 0-8306-5841-6.

Heiserman, David L., *Robot Intelligence with Experiments*, Tab, 1981, ISBN 0-8306-1191-6.

Heiserman, David L., *How to Design & Build Your Own Custom Robot*, Tab, 1981, ISBN 0-8306-1341-3.

Hero, of Alexandria *Automata*, 50 AD (?)

Higgins, Mike, *A Robot in Every Home, An Introduction to Personal Robots & Brand Name Buyer's Guide*, Kensington, 1985, ISBN 0-931445-17-7.

Holland, John M. *Designing Autonomous Mobile Robots: Inside the Mind of an Intelligent Machine* Newnes 2003, ISBN-10: 0750676833.

Hubbard, John D.; Larsen, Lawrence P. *Hero 2000 - Programming and Interfacing*, Heathkit/Zenith 1986. ISBN 0871191539.

Iagnemma, Karl; Dubowsky, Steven *Mobile Robots in Rough Terrain: Estimation, Motion Planning, and Control with Application to Planetary Rovers*, Springer, ISBN-10: 3642060269.

Imahara, Grant *Kickin' Bot: An Illustrated Guide to Building Combat Robots*, 1st ed, 2003, ISBN-0764541137.

Jones, Joseph L; Seiger, Bruce A.; Flynn, Anita A. *Mobile Robots: Inspiration to Implementation*, Second Edition, A K Peters/CRC Press; 2nd edition, 1998), ISBN-1568810970.

Kachroo, Pushkin and Mellodge, Patricia *Mobile Robotic Car Design* McGraw-Hill/TAB Electronics; 1st edition, 2004, ISBN-007143870X.

Kelly, Alonzo *Mobile Robotics,* Cambridge University Press; 1st edition, 2014, ASIN: B00E99YN9C.

Kent, Ernest W. *The Brains of Men and Machines*, 1981, Byte Mc-Graw-Hill, ISBN 0-07-034123-0.

Kortenkamp, David (Ed); Bonasso, R Peter (Ed), Murphy, Robin R. (Ed) *Bonasso Artificial Intelligence and Mobile Robots: Case Studies of Successful Robot System* AAAI Press; 1st edition, 1998, ISBN-0262611376.

Knight, Timothy Orr *Probots and People: The Age of the Personal Robot*, 1984, McGraw Hill, ISBN 0070351066.

Kurt, Tod E. *Hacking Roomba*, 2006, Wiley, ISBN 0470072717 .

Jones, Joseph L; Seiger, Bruce A.; Flynn, Anita M. *Mobile Robots: Inspiration to Implementation, Second Edition,* A K Peters/CRC Press; 2nd ed, 1998, ISBN- 1568810970 .

Lonergan, Tom and Frederick, Carl, *The VOR (Volitionally Operant Robot*, Hayden, 1983, ISBN 0-8104-5186-7.

Loofbourrow, Tod, *How to Build a Computer Controlled Robot*, Hayden, 1978, ISBN 0-8104-5681-8.

Malone, Robert, *The Robot Book*, PushPin Press, 1978, ISBN 0-15-678452-1.

Margolis, Michael *Make an Arduino-Controlled Robot,* Maker Media, Inc; 1st ed, 2012, ISBN-1449344372.

Marrs, Texe, *The Personal Robot Book,* Tab, 1985, ISBN 0-8306-1896-1.

Martin, Fred; Silverman, Brian, *"The Handy Logo Reference Manual,"* Jan 12, 1996, MIT Media Lab. http://cs.wellesley.edu/rds/handouts/HandyLogoReferenceManual.pdf

Miles, Peter and Carroll *Build your Own Combat Robot*, 2002, Mc-Graw Hill/Osborne, ISBN 0072194642 .

Miller, Merl K., Winkless, Nels, and Bosworth, Joe *Personal Robot Navigator*, 1999, A K Peters, ISBN 188819300X.

Moravec, Hans; *Mind Children, The Future of Robot and Human Intelligence*, 1988, Harvard University Press, ISBN 0-674-57618-7.

Moravec, Hans *The Stanford Cart and the CMU Rover*, Feb 24, 1983, Robotics Institute, Carnegie Mellon University, AD-A133207.

Mukhar, Kevin and Johnson, Dave *The Ultimate Palm Robot*, 2003, Osborne McGraw Hill, ISBN 0072228806.

Nonami, Kenzo; Kendoul, Farid; Suzuki, Satoshi; Wang, Wei; Nakazawa, Daisuke *Autonomous Flying Robots: Unmanned Aerial Vehicles and Micro Aerial Vehicles,* Springer, 2010, ISBN 4431538550.

Nourbakhsh, Illah Reza; Scaramuzza, Davide; Siegwart, Ronald *Introduction to Autonomous Mobile Robots*, 2nd edition, 2011, TBS, 2011, ISBN-8120343220.

Osborne, David M., *Robots, an Introduction to Basic Concepts and Applications*, Midwest Sci-Tech, 1983, ISBN 0-910853-00-2.

Osborne, David M., *Robots, the Application of Robots to Practical Work*, Midwest Sci-Tech, 1984, ISBN 0-910853-03-7.

Papert, Seymour "*Mind Storms, Children, Computers, and Powerful Ideas*," 1980, ISBN 0465046746.

Prochnow, David *The Official Robosapien Hacker's Guide*, 2005, McGraw Hill/Tab, ISBN 0071463097.

Raucci, Richard, *Personal Robotics: Real Robots to Construct, Program, and Explore the World*, 1999, CRC Press, ISBN 9781568810898.

The RB5X Reference Manual, RB Robot Corp, Golden, CO, 1983,

The RB Arm Documentation, RB Robot Corp, Golden, CO, Nov. 1983,

RB5X Voice/Sound Synthesis Package, RB Robot Corp, Golden, CO, Nov. 1983.

Reichardt, Jasia, *Robots, Fact, Fiction, & Prediction*", Penguin, 1978, ISBN 0-14-00.4938X.

Robillard, Mark J. "*Microprocessor Based Robotics*", Sams, 1983, ISBN 0-672-22050-

Robillard, Mark J. "*Advanced Robotic Systems*," 1984, Sams, ISBN 0672221667.

Robillard, Mark J. *HERO 1 - Advanced Programming and Interfacing*, H.W. Sams 1983. ISBN 0672221659.

Rosheim, Mark *Leonardo's Lost Robots*, 2006, Springer, ISBN-3540284400.

Safford, Edward L. Jr., *Handbook of Advanced Robotics*, Tab, 1982, ISBN 0-8306-1421-4.

Seigwart, Roland, Nourbakhsh, Illah Reza; Scaramuzza, Davide *Introduction to Autonomous Mobile Robots* (Intelligent Robotics and Autonomous Agents series), The MIT Press; 2nd edition, 2011, ISBN-0262015358.

Shea, Therese *The Robotics Club: Teaming up to Build Robots*, 2011, Rosen Central 1448812372.

Stakem, Patrick H. "R2-D2: A PC-Powered Mobile Robot," *Servo* magazine, March 2005, V3 n3.

Stakem, P. and Hynes, S. "Robot Hand Sensors for Object Location and Manipulation," with S. Hynes, IPRC-2, September 1985.

Stakem, Patrick H. "Use of Zero-power Ram for Personal Robots", *Robot Experimenter Magazine*, Aug. 1985.

Stakem, Patrick H. "Keeping the Hero-1 Robot's Wheel Straight,"*Robotics Age*, Feb. 1985.

Stakem, Patrick H. and Hynes, S. "Sensors for Robots, the Integration of Sensed Data, and Knowledge-Based Navigation Systems,", IPRC-1, Albuquerque, NM, April 1984.

Stakem, Patrick H. "Comparison of Information Content of Biological and Digital Systems," *Byte*, February 1979.

Stone, Brad *Gearheads: The Turbulent Rise of Robotic Sports*, 2003, Simon & Schuster, ISBN 0743229517.

Swigwart, Roland and Nourbakhsh, Illah R. *Introduction to Autonomous Mobile Robots (Intelligent Robotics and Autonomous Agents)* MIT Press; 2004, ISBN 026219502X.

Tzafestas, Spyros G. *Introduction to Mobile Robot Control*, Elsevier; 1st ed, 2013, ASIN: B00G4N7JLA, ISBN: 0124170498.

Tzafestas, Spyros G. (ed) *Web-Based Control and Robotics Education*, Springer, 2009, ISBN-1 9048125049.

Tzafestas, Spyros G. *Advances in Intelligent Autonomous Systems,* Kluwer Academic; 1999 ed , 1999, ISBN-0792355806.

Weinstein, Martin Bradley, *Android Design, Practical Approaches for Robot Builders*, Hayden, 1981, ISBN 0-8104-5192-1.

Williams, Doug *PDA Robotics*, 2003, McGraw Hill/Tab, ISBN 0071417419.

Winkless, Nels and Browning, Iben, *Robots on Your Doorstep*, Robotics Press, 1978, ISBN 0-89661-000-4.

Winkless III, Nelson B., *If I Had A Robot...What to Expect from the Personal Robot*, dilithium Press, 1984, ISBN 0-88056-353-2.

Wikipedia, various. Material from Wikipedia (www.wikipedia.org) is used under the conditions of the Creative commons Attribution-ShareAlike #.0 Unported License.

Industrial Robots

Albus, James & Evans, *"Robot Systems"*, Scientific American, Feb. 1976.

Albus, James S., Berbera, Anthony J., and Nazel, Roger N., *"Theory and Practice of Hierarchical Control"*, Twenty Third IEEE Computer Society International Conference, Sept. 1981.

Barbera, A., *"An Architecture for a Robot Hierarchical Control System"*, NBS Pub. 500-23, 1977.

Bloom, Howard M., Furlani, Cita M., and Berbera, Anthony J., *"Emulation as a Design Tool in the Development of Real-Time Control Systems"*, 1984 Winter Simulation Conference, Dallas, TX, Nov. 28-30, 1984.

Borenstein, J.; Everett, H. R.; Feng, Ligiang, *Navigation Mobile Robots: Systems and Techniques*, 1996, AK Peters, ISBN 156881058X.
Brady, Michael, Hollerbach, John M., Johnson, Timothy L., Lozano-Perez, Tomas, Mason, Matthew T. (ed), *Robot Motion Planning and Control*, MIT Press, 1982, ISBN 0-262-02182-X.

Braunl, Thomas *Embedded Robotics: Mobile Robot Design and Applications with Embedded Systems,* Springer; 2003, ISBN-10: 35400343.

D'Ignazio, Fred, *Working Robots*, Hayden, 1984, ISBN 0-8104- .

Engelberger, Joseph F. *Robots in Service*, 1989, MIT Press, ISBN 0262050420.

Evans, Albus, James; Barbera,Anthony *"NBS/RIA Workshop Proceedings"*, 1977, NBS 500-29

Goto, T., Inoyama, T., and Takeyasu, K., "Precise insert operation by tactile controlled robots." 4th International Symposium on Industrial Robots, Tokyo, 1974.

Gottlieb, Irving M., *Electric Motors & Control Techniques*, Tab, 1982, ISBN 0-8306-2565-8.

Heath Company, Benton Harbor, MI.

   "Industrial Electronics & Automation", EB-1903

   "Robot Applications", EE-1812

   "Robotics & Industrial Electronics", EE-1800

Herman, Martin, "*Fast, Three-Dimensional, Collision-Free Motion Planning*", Proc. 1986 IEEE International Conference on Robotics and Automation, April 7-10, 1986, San Francisco.

IEEE Proceedings, July 1983, Special Issue on Robotics, Vol. 71, No. 7.

Kent, Ernest W., and Albus, James S., *Servoed World Models as Interfaces Between Robot Control System and Sensing Data*, Robotica (1984) Vol. 2 pp. 17-25.

Korf, "*Space Robotics*", Carnegie-Mellon University, Robotics Institute, CMU-RI-TR-82-10.

Lee, Gonzalez, Fu, "*Tutorial on Robotics*", IEEE, 1983, IEEE Computer Society. order number 515.

Lumia, Ronald, "*Representing Solids for a Real-Time Robot Sensory System*", NBS.

Madhavan, Raj Messina, Elana R. and Albus, James Sacra *Intelligent Vehicle Systems: A 4D/RCS Approach*, Nova Science Publishers (January 15, 2007. ISBN-10: 1600212603.

Michael E. Moran. *The da Vinci robot*, Journal of Endourology. December 2006, Volume:20 Issue 12: January 5, 2007

NASA, *Interface Design Considerations for Robotic Satellite Servicers*, Nov. 1989, JSC 23920, NASA, Johnson Space Flight Center.

NASA, SS-GSFC-0027, "*NASA/NBS Standard Reference Model for Telerobot Control System Architecture*", 6/18/87, NASA – Goddard Space Flight Center.

NASA, *FTS In-House Phase B Study TINMAN Concept*, Feb. 12, 1988, NASA GSFC.

NBS, *Overview of Artificial Intelligence and Robotics, Vol. 2, Robotics*, National Bureau of Standards, Mar. 82, PB83-217547.

NBS document ICG-002, "*Manipulator Servo Level Task Decomposition*", John Fiala, 12/87.

NBS Document ICG-004, "*Interfaces to Teleoperation Devices*", John Fiala, 12/87.

NBS Document ICG-003, "*Manipulator Primitive Level Task Decomposition*", Albert J. Wavering, Jan. 1988.

Paul, R.P., and Shimano, B., "*Compliance and Control*", Joint Automatic Control Conference, Purdue University, July 1976.

Raibert, M.H., and Craig, J.J., "Hybrid Position/Force Control of Manipulators", ASME, Journal of Dynamic Systems, Measurement, and Control, Volume 102, June 1981; also in Robot Motion, Planning, and Control, pp. 419-438, Brady, Hollerbach, Johnson, Lozano-Perez, and Mason, eds., Cambridge, Mass., M.I.T. Press, 1983.

Rodriguez (ed), "Proceedings of the Workshop on Space Telerobotics", 3 Vol., July 1, 1987, JPL 87-13.

Salisbury, J. K., "Active Stiffness Control of a Manipulator in Cartesian Coordinates", 19th IEEE Conference on Decision and Control, December 1980.

Shimano, B., and Roth, B., "*On Force Sensing Information and Its Use in Controlling Manipulators*", pp 119-126, Eighth International Symposium on Industrial Robots, Japan.

Snyder, Wesley E., *Industrial Robots: Computer Interfacing and Control*, Prentice-Hall, 1985, ISBN 0-13-463159-5.

Stakem, Patrick "Advanced Computational Architecture for Flight Telerobotic Servicers", Satellite Services Workshop IV, June 21-23, 1988, Johnson Space Center, Texas.

Stakem, Patrick H. "The Brilliant Bulldozer: Parallel Processing Techniques for Onboard Computation in Unmanned Vehicles", 15th AUVS Symposium, San Diego, Ca. June 6-8, 1988.

Stakem, Pat; Lumia, Ron; Smith, Dave; "A Computer and Communications Architecture for the Flight Telerobotic Servicer," June 24, 1988, ICG-#20, Intelligent Controls Group, Robot Systems Division, National Bureau of Standards.

Takase, K.H., Inoue, K., and Hagiwara, S., "The design of an articulated manipulator with torque control ability", 4th International Symposium on Industrial Robots, IIT, Chicago, Sept. 1975.

Tanner, William R. *Industrial Robots Fundamentals*, SME, 1979, ASIN: B000ICNS7C.

Whitney, D. E., "*Force Feedback Control of Manipulator Fine Motions*", ASME, Journal of Dynamic Systems, Measurement, and Control, June 1977.

Wu, C.H., and Paul, R.P., "Resolved Motion Force Control of Robot Manipulator", IEEE Transactions on Systems, Man, and Cybernetics, Volume SMC-12, Number 3, June 1982.

Young, John Frederick "*Robotics*", Halsted Press (Wiley), 1973, ISBN 0408705221 .

Selected Bibliography on Embedded Systems, applicable to Robotics

Analog Devices, *Analog-Digital Conversion Handbook*, Prentice-Hall, 3rd ed, 1986, ISBN 0-13-032848-0.

Arnold, Ken *Embedded Controller Hardware Design*, Newnes; 1 edition, 2001, ISBN-1878707523.

Ball, Stuart, *Embedded Microprocessor Systems: Real World Design*, 3rd ed, Newnes, 2002, ISBN 0-0-7506-7534-9.

Ball, Stuart, *Analog Interfacing to Embedded Microprocessors, Real World Design*, 2nd ed, Newnes, 2004, ISBN 1-878-70798-1.

Ball, Stuart, *Debugging Embedded Microprocessor Systems*, Newnes; 1st edition, 1998, ISBN 0750699906

Berger, Arnold S. *Embedded Systems Design: An Introduction to Processes, Tools and Techniques*, CMP Books, 2001, ISBN- 978-1578200733.

DeMuth, Brian and Eisenreich, Dan *Designing Embedded Internet Devices*, Newnes, 2002, ISBN 1878707981.

Doboli, Alex and Currie, Edward H. *Introduction to Mixed-Signal, Embedded Design,* Springer, 2010 ISBN- 1441974458.

Eady, Fred *Implementing 802.11 with Microcontrollers: Wireless Networking for Embedded Systems Designers*, Newnes, 2005, ISBN 0750678658.

Edwards, Lewin *Embedded System Design on a Shoestring Achieving High Performance with a Limited Budget*, Newnes, 2003, ISBN 0750676094.

Edwards, Lewin *Open-Source Robotics and Process Control Cookbook: Designing and Building Robust, Dependable Real-time Systems,* Newnes, 2004, ISBN- 0750677783.

Eskandarian, Azim (Ed) *Handbook of Intelligent Vehicles* Springer; 2012 edition, ISBN- 085729086X.

Fraden, Jacob *Handbook of Modern Sensors: Physics, Designs, and Applications* Springer; 3rd edition (December 4, 2003) ISBN-0387007504.

Fowler, Kim R. *What Every Engineer Should Know About Developing Real-Time Embedded Products*, CRC Press, 2007, ISBN- 0849379598.

Ganssle, Jack; Noergaard, Tammy; Eady, Fred; and Edwards, Lewin; *Embedded Hardware*, Newnes, 2007, ISBN-978-0750685849.

Ganssle, Jack, *The Art of Designing Embedded Systems* (EDN Series for Design Engineers) Newnes, 1999, ISBN-978-0750698696.

Ganssle, Jack and Barr, Mike *Embedded Systems Dictionary*, CMP; 1st edition, 2003, ISBN- 1578201209.

Heath, Steve, *Embedded Systems Design, Second Ed,* Newnes; 2 edition, 2002, ISBN-0750655461.

Ienne, Paolo and Leupers, Rainer *Customizable Embedded Processors Design Technologies and Applications*, Morgan Kaufmann; 1st edition, 2006, ISBN-0123695260.

Kalinsky, David, *Architecture of Safety-Critical Systems*, http://www.embedded.com/columns/technicalinsights/169600396.

Kleman, Alan *Interfacing Microprocessors in Hydraulic Systems,* CRC Press 1st. ed, 1989, ISBN 0824780639.

Koopman, Philip "Embedded System Security," IEEE Computer, July 2004.

Kornaros, Georgios *Multi-Core Embedded Systems,* CRC Press, 2012, ASIN B008KZBZL0.

Lee, Insup (ed), *Handbook of Real-Time and Embedded Systems,* Chapman and Hall/CRC, 2007, ISBN- 1584886781.

Leveson, Nancy G. *System Safety and Computers,* Addison-Wesley, 1995, ISBN: 0-201-11972-2.

Li, Qing and Yao, Caroline *Real-Time Concepts for Embedded Systems,* CMP; 1st edition, 2003, ISBN- 1578201241.

Martinez, David R. (ed) et al *High Performance Embedded Computing Handbook: A Systems Perspective* CRC Press; 1st edition, 2008, ISBN- 084937197X.

Matalon, Shabtay, et al "Embedded System Power Consumption: A Software or Hardware issue?" Mentor Graphics.

Noergaard, Tammy, *Embedded Systems Architecture: A Comprehensive Guide for Engineers and Programmers,* Newnes, 2005, ISBN-978-0750677929.

Ortiz, David A. and Santiago, Nayda G. *High-Level Optimization for Low Power Consumption on Microprocessor-Based Systems,* 2007, IEEE 1-4244-1176-9/07.

Parab, Jivan et al, *Practical Aspects of Embedded System Design using Microcontrollers,* Springer; Softcover reprint of hardcover 1st ed. 2008 edition, 2010, ISBN: 9048178657.

Simone, Lisa *If I Only Changed the Software, Why is the Phone on Fire?: Embedded Debugging Methods Revealed Technical Mysteries for Engineers,* Newnes, 2007, ISBN 0750682183.

Smith, Warwick A. *Arm Microcontroller Interfacing,* Elektor International, 2010, ISBN- 0905705912.

Spaanenburg, Lambert and Spaanenburg, Hendrik, *Cloud Connectivity and Embedded Sensory Systems,* Springer; 1st Edition, 2010, ISBN-1441975446.

Stapko, Timothy *Practical Embedded Security: Building Secure Resource-Constrained Systems,* Newnes; 1st edition, 2007, ISBN-: 0750682159.

Storey, Neil *Safety-Critical Computer Systems,* Addison-Wesley, 1996. ISBN: 0-201-42787-7.

Truszkowski, Walt *Autonomous and Autonomic Systems: With Applications to NASA Intelligent Spacecraft Operations and Exploration Systems,* Springer; 1st Edition. edition, 2009, ISBN-1846282322.

Vahid, Frank and Givargis, Tony D., *Embedded System Design: A Unified Hardware/Software Introduction,* Wiley, 2001, ISBN-978-0471386780.

Valvano, Jonathan W. *Embedded Microcomputer Systems: Real Time Interfacing,* Cengage-Engineering, 2006, ISBN- 978-0534551629.

Valvano, Jonathan W. *Embedded systems: Real time Interfacing to the ARM Cortex-M3,* CreateSpace Independent Publishing Platform, November 10, 2011, ISBN- 1463590156.

Valvano, Jonathan W. *Embedded systems: Real-Time Operating systems for the ARM Cortex-M3,* CreateSpace Independent Publishing Platform, January 3, 2012, ISBN- 1466468866.

White, Elecia *Making Embedded Systems,* O'Reilly Media, 2011, ASIN B005ZTO0LG.

Williams, Al *Embedded Internet Design* McGraw-Hill/TAB Electronics; 1st edition (March 12, 2003) ISBN-10071374361.

Wilson, Graham R. *Embedded Systems & Computer Architecture,* Newnes, 2002, ASIN: B008AUG2U4.

Wolf, Marilyn *Computers As Components, Principles of Embedded Computing System Design,* Publisher: Morgan Kaufmann; 3rd edition, 2012, ISBN 978-0-12-388436-7.

Wolf, Wayne, *High-Performance Embedded Computing: Architectures, Applications, and Methodologies,* Morgan Kaufmann, 2006, ISBN- 978-0123694850.

The Concise Handbook of Real-Time Systems, TimeSys Corp., www.timesys.com

Operating systems

Android

Gargenta, Marko *Learning Android* O'Reilly Media; 1st edition, 2011, ISBN- 1449390501.

Milette, Greg and Stroud, Adam *Professional Android Sensor Programming*, Wrox, 1st edition, 2012, ISBN- 1118183487.

Steele, James and To, Nelson *The Android Developer's Cookbook: Building Applications with the Android SDK: Building Applications with the Android SDK* (Developer's Library), Addison-Wesley Professional; 1st edition, 2010, ISBN- 0321741234.

Yaghmour, Karim *Embedded Android: Porting, Extending, and Customizing* O'Reilly Media, 2012, ISBN- 144930829.

Gnu/Linux and BSD

Abbott, Doug, *Linux for Embedded and Real-time Applications* (2nd Edition), Newnes; 2nd edition, 2006, ISBN 0750679328.

Cevoli, Paul *Embedded FreeBSD Cookbook*, Newnes, 2002, ISBN 1589950046.

Hallinan, Christopher *Embedded Linux Primer: A Practical Real-World Approach,* Prentice Hall PTR; 1 edition, 2006, ISBN- 0131679848.

Hollabaugh, Craig; *Embedded Linux: Hardware, Software, and Interfacing*, Addison-Wesley Professional; 1st edition, 2002, ISBN- 0672322269.

Lombardo, John *Embedded Linux*, New Riders Publishing, 2001, ISBN 0-7357-0998-X.

Nicholson, J. *Starting Embedded Linux Development on an ARM Architecture*, Newnes. July 2013, ISBN 9780080982366.

Raghavan, P. *Embedded Linux System Design and Development*, Auerbach, 2005, ISBN- 978-0849340581.

Yaghmour, Karim *Building Embedded Linux Systems,* O'Reilly Media, Inc.; 1st edition, 2003, ISBN- 059600222X.

www.Linuxdevices.com

www.elks.sourceforge.net

Freebsd architecture handbook
 http://www.freebsd.org/doc/en/books/arch-handbook/

POSIX
 http://standards.ieee.org/develop/wg/POSIX.html

QNX

Hildebrand, Dan "An Architectural Overview of QNX". Proceedings of the Workshop on Micro-kernels and Other Kernel Architectures," 1992, pp 113–126. ISBN 1-880446-42-1.

Embedded Software and Programming
Barr, Michael; Massa, Anthony; *Programming Embedded Systems: With C and GNU Development Tools*, 2nd Edition O'Reilly Media, Inc.; 2nd edition, 2006, ISBN-0596009836.

Bentley, Jon Louis, *Writing Efficient Programs*, 1982 Prentice Hall, ISBN 0139702512.

Chisnall, David "Optimizing Code for Power Consumption," Nov. 18, 2010, Addison-Wesley Professional, www.informit.com/articles/

Cofer, R. C. and Harding Benjamin F. *Rapid System Programming with FPGA's*, 2006, Newnes Elsevier, ISBN 0-7506-7866-6.

Curtis, Keith E. *Embedded Multitasking*, Newnes, 2006, ISBN 0750679182.

Ganssle, Jack *The Art of Programming Embedded Systems* Publisher: Academic Press; 1st edition, 1991, ISBN 0122748808.

Ganssle, Jack *Embedded Systems, World Class Designs*, Newnes; 1st edition, 2007, ISBN- 0750686251.

Kamal, Raj *Embedded Systems: Architecture, Programming and Design*, 2nd Edition McGraw-Hill Education (India); 2nd Edition, 2009, ISBN 0070151253.

Labrosse, Jean J.; Ganssle, Jack; Oshana, Robert; Walls, Colin; *Embedded Software*, Newnes, 200,7 ISBN-978-0750685832, ASINB007N1KOCI.

Lamie, Edward *Real-Time Embedded Multithreading Using ThreadX and ARM*, Newnes; 2nd edition, 2009, ISBN 1856176010.

Leveson, Nancy G. "Software Safety in Embedded Computer Systems," Communications of the ACM. Vol. 34, No. 2, February 1991, pp. 34-46.

Lewis, David W. *Fundamentals of Embedded Software: Where C and Assembly Meet*, Prentice Hall; 1st edition, 2001, ISBN 0130615897.

Lewis, David W. *Fundamentals of Embedded Software with the ARM Cortex-M3*, Prentice Hall; 1st edition, February 12, 2012, ISBN- 0132916541.

Morgan, Sara *Programming Microsoft Robotics Studio*, 2008, Microsoft Press, ISBN 0735624321.

Murphy, Niall *Front Panel: Designing Software for Embedded User Interfaces*, CMP; 1st edition, 1998, ISBN 0879305282.

Simon, David E. *An Embedded Software Primer*, Addison-Wesley Professional, 199), ISBN 020161569X.

Sridhar, T. *Designing Embedded Communications Software*, Publisher: CMP; 1st edition, 2003, ISBN: 157820125X.

Wichmann, Brian A. *Software in Safety Related Systems*, Wiley, 1992. ISBN 0471-93474-7.

Motor and Device Control

Herman, Stephen L. *Understanding Motor Controls* Delmar Cengage Learning; 1 edition (August 4, 2005), ISBN 1401890164.

Kenjo, Takashi and Sugawara, Akira *Stepping Motors and Their Microprocessor Controls* Oxford University Press, USA; 2 edition (January 15, 1994), ISBN 0198593856.
Patrick, Dale R. and Fardo, Stephen W. *Laboratory Manual for Electrical Motor Control Systems: Electronic and Digital Controls*

Fundamentals and Applications Goodheart-Willcox Co (January 1, 2000), ISBN 1566377021.

Petruzella, Frank *Electric Motors and Control Systems* Career Education; 1 edition (May 8, 2009), ISBN 0073521825.

Pfister, Cuno *Getting Started with the Internet of Things: Connecting Sensors and Microcontrollers to the Cloud*, O'Reilly Media; 1st edition, June 2, 2011, ISBN- 1449393578.

Rockis, Gary J. and Mazur, Glen A. *Electrical Motor Controls for Integrated Systems*
Amer Technical Pub; 4 edition (January 1, 2009), ISBN 0826912176.

Valentine, Richard *Motor Control Electronics Handbook*, 1998, McGraw-Hill Professional; ISBN 0070668108.

Device Interfacing

Fischer-Cripps, Tony *Newnes Interfacing Companion: Computers, Transducers, Instrumentation and Signal Processing* Newnes (December 20, 2002), ISBN 0750657200.

Valvano, Jonathan W. *Introduction to Embedded Systems: Interfacing to the Freescale 9S12* CL-Engineering; 1 edition (April 23, 2009), ISBN 049541137X.

Resources
www.theoldrobots.com

If you enjoyed this book, you might also be interested in some of these.

Stakem, Patrick H. *16-bit Microprocessors, History and Architecture*, 2013 PRRB Publishing, ISBN-1520210922.

Stakem, Patrick H. *4- and 8-bit Microprocessors, Architecture and History*, 2013, PRRB Publishing, ISBN-152021572X,

Stakem, Patrick H. *Apollo's Computers,* 2014, PRRB Publishing, ISBN-1520215800.

Stakem, Patrick H. *The Architecture and Applications of the ARM Microprocessors,* 2013, PRRB Publishing, ISBN-1520215843.

Stakem, Patrick H. *Earth Rovers: for Exploration and Environmental Monitoring,* 2014, PRRB Publishing, ISBN-152021586X.

Stakem, Patrick H. *Embedded Computer Systems, Volume 1, Introduction and Architecture,* 2013, PRRB Publishing, ISBN-1520215959.

Stakem, Patrick H. *The History of Spacecraft Computers from the V-2 to the Space Station*, 2013, PRRB Publishing, ISBN-1520216181.

Stakem, Patrick H. *Floating Point Computation*, 2013, PRRB Publishing, ISBN-152021619X.

Stakem, Patrick H. *Architecture of Massively Parallel Microprocessor Systems*, 2011, PRRB Publishing, ISBN-1520250061.

Stakem, Patrick H. *Multicore Computer Architecture*, 2014, PRRB Publishing, ISBN-1520241372.

Stakem, Patrick H. *Personal Robots*, 2014, PRRB Publishing, ISBN-1520216254.

Stakem, Patrick H. *RISC Microprocessors, History and Overview*, 2013, PRRB Publishing, ISBN-1520216289.

Stakem, Patrick H. *Robots and Telerobots in Space Applications*, 2011, PRRB Publishing, ISBN-1520210361.

Stakem, Patrick H. *The Saturn Rocket and the Pegasus Missions, 1965*, 2013, PRRB Publishing, ISBN-1520209916.

Stakem, Patrick H. *Visiting the NASA Centers, and Locations of Historic Rockets & Spacecraft*, 2017, PRRB Publishing, ISBN-1549651205.

Stakem, Patrick H. *Microprocessors in Space*, 2011, PRRB Publishing, ISBN-1520216343.

Stakem, Patrick H. Computer *Virtualization and the Cloud*, 2013, PRRB Publishing, ISBN-152021636X.

Stakem, Patrick H. *What's the Worst That Could Happen? Bad Assumptions, Ignorance, Failures and Screw-ups in Engineering Projects, 2014,* PRRB Publishing, ISBN-1520207166.

Stakem, Patrick H. *Computer Architecture & Programming of the Intel x86 Family, 2013,* PRRB Publishing, ISBN-1520263724.

Stakem, Patrick H. *The Hardware and Software Architecture of the Transputer,* 2011,PRRB Publishing, ISBN-152020681X.

Stakem, Patrick H. *Mainframes, Computing on Big Iron,* 2015, PRRB Publishing, ISBN- 1520216459.

Stakem, Patrick H. *Spacecraft Control Centers,* 2015, PRRB Publishing, ISBN-1520200617.

Stakem, Patrick H. *Embedded in Space,* 2015, PRRB Publishing, ISBN-1520215916.

Stakem, Patrick H. *A Practitioner's Guide to RISC Microprocessor Architecture,* Wiley-Interscience, 1996, ISBN-0471130184.

Stakem, Patrick H. *Cubesat Engineering,* PRRB Publishing, 2017, ISBN-1520754019.

Stakem, Patrick H. *Cubesat Operations,* PRRB Publishing, 2017, ISBN-152076717X.

Stakem, Patrick H. *Interplanetary Cubesats,* PRRB Publishing, 2017, ISBN-1520766173 .

Stakem, Patrick H. Cubesat Constellations, Clusters, and Swarms, Stakem, PRRB Publishing, 2017, ISBN-1520767544.

Stakem, Patrick H. *Graphics Processing Units, an overview*, 2017, PRRB Publishing, ISBN-1520879695.

Stakem, Patrick H. *Intel Embedded and the Arduino-101, 2017,* PRRB Publishing, ISBN-1520879296.

Stakem, Patrick H. *Orbital Debris, the problem and the mitigation,* 2018, PRRB Publishing, ISBN-*1980466483*.

Stakem, Patrick H. *Manufacturing in Space,* 2018, PRRB Publishing, ISBN-1977076041.

Stakem, Patrick H. *NASA's Ships and Planes,* 2018, PRRB Publishing, ISBN-1977076823.

Stakem, Patrick H. *Space Tourism,* 2018, PRRB Publishing, ISBN-1977073506.

Stakem, Patrick H. *STEM – Data Storage and Communications,* 2018, PRRB Publishing, ISBN-1977073115.

Stakem, Patrick H. *In-Space Robotic Repair and Servicing,* 2018, PRRB Publishing, ISBN-1980478236.

Stakem, Patrick H. *Introducing Weather in the pre-K to 12 Curricula, A Resource Guide for Educators,* 2017, PRRB Publishing, ISBN-1980638241.

Stakem, Patrick H. *Introducing Astronomy in the pre-K to 12 Curricula, A Resource Guide for Educators,* 2017, PRRB Publishing, ISBN-198104065X.

Also available in a Brazilian Portuguese edition, ISBN-1983106127.

Stakem, Patrick H. *Deep Space Gateways, the Moon and Beyond*, 2017, PRRB Publishing, ISBN-1973465701.

Stakem, Patrick H. *Exploration of the Gas Giants, Space Missions to Jupiter, Saturn, Uranus, and Neptune*, PRRB Publishing, 2018, ISBN-9781717814500.

Stakem, Patrick H. *Crewed Spacecraft*, 2017, PRRB Publishing, ISBN-1549992406.

Stakem, Patrick H. *Rocketplanes to Space*, 2017, PRRB Publishing, ISBN-1549992589.

Stakem, Patrick H. *Crewed Space Stations*, 2017, PRRB Publishing, ISBN-1549992228.

Stakem, Patrick H. *Enviro-bots for STEM: Using Robotics in the pre-K to 12 Curricula, A Resource Guide for Educators*, 2017, PRRB Publishing, ISBN-1549656619.

Stakem, Patrick H. *STEM-Sat, Using Cubesats in the pre-K to 12 Curricula, A Resource Guide for Educators*, 2017, ISBN-1549656376.

Stakem, Patrick H. *Lunar Orbital Platform-Gateway*, 2018, PRRB Publishing, ISBN-1980498628.

Stakem, Patrick H. *Embedded GPU's*, 2018, PRRB Publishing, ISBN- 1980476497.

Stakem, Patrick H. *Mobile Cloud Robotics*, 2018, PRRB Publishing, ISBN- 1980488088.

Stakem, Patrick H. *Extreme Environment Embedded Systems,* 2017, PRRB Publishing, ISBN-1520215967.

Stakem, Patrick H. *What's the Worst, Volume-2*, 2018, ISBN-1981005579.

Stakem, Patrick H., *Spaceports*, 2018, ISBN-1981022287.

Stakem, Patrick H., *Space Launch Vehicles*, 2018, ISBN-1983071773.

Stakem, Patrick H. *Mars*, 2018, ISBN-1983116902.

Stakem, Patrick H. *X-86, 40th Anniversary ed*, 2018, ISBN-1983189405.

Stakem, Patrick H. *Lunar Orbital Platform-Gateway*, 2018, PRRB Publishing, ISBN-1980498628.

Stakem, Patrick H. *Space Weather*, 2018, ISBN-1723904023.

Stakem, Patrick H. *STEM-Engineering Process*, 2017, ISBN-1983196517.

Stakem, Patrick H. *Space Telescopes,* 2018, PRRB Publishing, ISBN-1728728568.

Stakem, Patrick H. *Exoplanets*, 2018, PRRB Publishing, ISBN-9781731385055.

Stakem, Patrick H. *Planetary Defense*, 2018, PRRB Publishing, ISBN-9781731001207.

Patrick H. Stakem *Exploration of the Asteroid Belt*, 2018, PRRB Publishing, ISBN-1731049846.

Patrick H. Stakem *Terraforming*, 2018, PRRB Publishing, ISBN-1790308100.

Patrick H. Stakem, *Martian Railroad,* 2019, PRRB Publishing, ISBN-1794488243.

Patrick H. Stakem, *Exoplanets,* 2019, PRRB Publishing, ISBN-1731385056.

Patrick H. Stakem, *Exploiting the Moon,* 2019, PRRB Publishing, ISBN-1091057850.

Patrick H. Stakem, *RISC-V, an Open Source Solution for Space Flight Computers,* 2019, PRRB Publishing, ISBN-1796434388.

Patrick H. Stakem, *Arm in Space*, 2019, PRRB Publishing, ISBN-9781099789137.

Patrick H. Stakem, *Extraterrestrial Life*, 2019, PRRB Publishing, ISBN-978-1072072188.

Stakem, Patrick H. Submarine Launched Ballistic Missiles, 2019, ISBN-978-1088954904.

Patrick H. Stakem, *Space Command*, 2019, PRRB Publishing, ISBN-978-1693005398.

www.ingramcontent.com/pod-product-compliance
Lightning Source LLC
LaVergne TN
LVHW092336060326
832902LV00008B/680